SETTING UP FAMILY GROUP PROJECTS:

A Practical Guide for Project Organisers Based on The Experience of COPE

Compiled by Mary Willis
Edited by Barbara Hearn

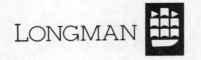

Published by Longman Industry and Public Service
Management, Longman Group UK Ltd, 6th Floor, Westgate
House, The High, Harlow, Essex CM20 1YR
Telephone Harlow (0279) 442601; Fax Harlow (0279) 444501; Telex
81491 Padlog

First published 1991

A catalogue record for this book is available from the British Library

ISBN 0-582-09142-X

Produced by Longman Group (FE) Ltd
Printed in Hong Kong

Contents

Foreword

This guide is based on the work of COPE, a small voluntary organisation which, over a 10-year period, enabled the setting-up of family groups in partnership with local agency workers and local people. COPE promoted the notion of family groups with agencies, and provided training and support to the agency staff and local people who became responsible for a number of family group projects in several localities.

Mary Willis was the General Secretary of COPE, and put together the material for this Guide so that the expertise built up by COPE could be made widely available. Mary worked with family group workers for 10 years and the compilation is based on 40 years of knowledge and experience. It was with the help and generosity of colleagues and the family group workers that Mary completed her work.

Acknowledgements

In preparing this text, I have to thank Ann Vandersypen, Nancy Dunlop, Nnennaya Onyekwere and Margaret Hogan for their persistent commitment. The initial support of Beth Morris, and the positive encouragement of Debbie Bowler who read the manuscript and gave me the confidence to believe it would be useful, were invaluable.

Without the original material provided by Mary Willis, and the support of the Department of Health, the opportunity to make available the experience of COPE and family groups to others would not have been possible.

Finally, thank you, as always, to Stephen and Beth for coping with me in the midst of the production.

Introduction: Why family groups?

Challenging isolation in neighbourhoods

This book is a guide to setting up family groups for, and with, people who have become isolated within a locality. A family group ensures that the caring which exists in that locality is focused and directed towards helping people whose capacity to cope with poverty, the care of their children, poor housing or just life is restricted by the lack of a caring network.

Recent research[1] has found that the isolation experienced by families is a factor in whether the risk of abuse to a child is increased. Yet, isolation as such is not a focal point for many workers directly responsible for protecting children. Whilst they may acknowledge its existence, playing a part in creating a caring network, and diminishing the damaging effects of isolation, is often not a priority. This guide offers a framework within which it is possible to take an active part in changing the circumstances of an isolated family or individual, and improving their quality of life. The reduction of risk through the existence of a reference group and support system is a crucial factor in favour of linking family groups to communities with a high incidence of family breakdown and a high need for help with child protection.

The legal context

The Children Act 1989 puts an emphasis upon partnership with parents, who, under this legislation, retain responsibility for parenting when they are in difficulty far more than previously. *The Children Act 1989* requires that local authorities, intervening in family life, in addition, prove that they have made every effort to retain the child within the family. They must also 'take reasonable steps . . . to prevent children within their area suffering ill treatment or neglect'. The threshold of intervention is thus raised. Hence, social workers will need to support and/or establish a range of community-based resources aimed at preventing family breakdown if they are to fulfil the spirit of the Act. The Act specifically mentions that local authorities 'shall provide' family centres, which are defined as places where parents, children and carers may 'attend for occupational, social, cultural or recreational activities'. Such functions are at the heart of family groups.

Local authorities, in collaboration with health, education, liaising and voluntary organisations, will need to develop preventative strategies. Rather than focusing on the crises when they occur, having a reactive style, agency staff will need to plan a way of anticipating demands, and develop resources proactively, in partnership with local people.

Family groups are a preventative resource which, when available to families in need, can reduce the demands coming to the agencies framed as crises. To achieve such a strategic approach will require a shift in attitudes. Prevention will need to be viewed as an activity as central as actioning legal proceedings or assessing abuse have been in the past. Performance indicators will have to change. This may mean re-educating politicians away from allocating resources on the basis of numbers of children on the protection register, or in care, towards the numbers of preventive places taken up by families, or to preventative services offered to them.

The local authority should not alone be responsible for such preventative resources as family groups. The DoH document *Working Together*[2] emphasises the need for inter-agency collaboration. This text highlights the tensions which can result but more importantly the need for collaboration in order to access the range of resources and skills needed to create successful family-group projects. Developing a family group can also be regarded as a promotional activity within the context of the *Community Care and NHS Act 1990*, which binds local authorities to promote the development of local resources.

What is a family-group project?

Family-group projects entail resource identification, a training programme, and finally the setting-up of family groups. Family-group projects do not discriminate on the basis of age, race, gender or disability. They are often composed of people who have various needs and who are of varied backgrounds. Isolated elders within a locality may have a great deal of expertise to offer the young parent and vice versa.

Family groups are at their most effective when clustered in a locality. To help crystallize the issues faced within family groups, Table 1.1 was drawn from a cluster of four groups in an urban area.

Table 1.1.

Group 1	Group 2
Depression	Severe depression
Agoraphobia	Alcoholism
Mental illness of spouse	Suspected child abuse
Isolation and loneliness	Isolation
Hyperactive child	Extreme shyness
Violence in the family	Handicap
Abortion	Widowhood
Repeated miscarriages	Divorce
Attempted suicide	Unemployment
A risk of child abuse	Difficult and disturbed children
Divorce	Infant feeding difficulties
	Marriage break-up
	Marital problems

Group 3	Group 4
Child abuse	Depression
Depression	Isolation
Ex-hospital patients	Loneliness
Bereavement	Shyness
Post-natal depression	Insecurity
Mixed race marriages	Bereavement
Newcomers	Single-parent problems
Abortion	Marital problems
Miscarriages	Divorce
Risk of child abuse	Child rearing difficulties
Poverty	Problem with step-children
Mental handicap	Poverty and low income
Isolation	
Husband in prison	

Several members experienced more than one problem, for example, many of the single parents were isolated and depressed with financial problems and with poor health.

Family groups have helped people to cope with the demands of caring for chronic illness and disability, mental illness and handicap, and with old age. They have given people increased knowledge about the problems of care, and information about the services available to provide help. They have shared some of the burdens of care, because members have helped each other in practical ways and because they have allowed each other to express their feelings of weariness or resentment and 'have a good moan'. The friendship networks, which the groups have helped to forge, continue to provide this help and support beyond sessions and ultimately beyond the life of the groups.

Family-group projects invariably are initiated and certainly are backed by statutory or voluntary organisations. Family groups themselves, though, are run by local people for local people. Once established, the face-to-face work undertaken by such bodies as local authority staff lessens. Family groups maintain the principle, established in research by Crosbie and Vickery[3], that successful community/local projects are led by local people and are not controlled centrally by agency staff. An example is given in Figure 1.1.

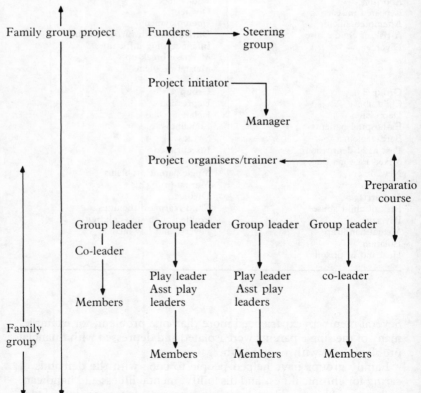

Fig. 1.1. A summary model of a family-group project.

Table 1.2 Relevance of family groups

Education	Health
• Educational opportunities for local people of all ages	• Informal 'where people are at' health education
• Training opportunities	• Development of positive self-health care
• Access to further education opportunities	• Take-up of preventive health care services
• Development of parenting skills	• Development of self-confidence as parents
• Bridge between parents and schools	• Information about health programmes

Housing	Social services
• Help with development of a sense of community	• Help with development of informal support networks
• Addressing of loneliness and isolation on large or 'labelled' estates	• Building of self-confidence and self-esteem
• Offer of a point for information gathering and sharing	• Nurture of self-help and mutual aid
• Help for people to understand their rights and responsibilities	• Development of parenting skills and control over own lives

Project benefits as seen by those involved

Politicians   'It openly recognises the strengths and skills of local people.'
'It releases resources within neighbourhoods.'
'Cost effective, preventive.'
'Puts an infra-structure into problem communities.'

Managers   'It enhances the work of my area.'
'It is something positive for me to offer.'
'It is well thought-out.'
'It is tried and proven.'
'It furthers the department's policies.'
'It can be supervised and measured.'

Project organisers   'It gives me the opportunity to develop new skills.'
'It gives me an 'in' to the neighbourhood.'

'It is a relief to do something that I can measure.'
'It has positive, concrete, visible outcomes.'
'It is an opportunity to work positively with local people.'

Local people 'It is an opportunity to learn and share.'
 'It is a job.'
 'It serves our community.'
 'It belongs to our community.'

Users 'It gives me friends.'
 'It gives me support.'
 'It is somewhere to go.'
 'It gives me strength.'
 'It is ours.'
 'It is fun.'
 'It helps.'

Some examples of projects

Family group projects have been achieved in Humberside, East Sussex, Bedford, Greater London, Kent, Devon, Runcorn, Widnes, Kirby, Wirral, Merseyside, Shropshire, and Leamington Spa.

Family group projects have been achieved by social services, education authorities, voluntary organisations, combinations of all three.

Family group projects have been successfully set up by social worker and day centre supervisor, social worker and family aide, social worker and social work assistant, social worker and residential centre worker, social worker and community worker, community education officers, community workers, community centre workers.

Family group projects can in addition be set up by staff of

- Social services: intermediate treatment workers, fostering officers, group workers
- Education: youth workers, education welfare officers
- Health: health visitors
- Housing: tenants' liaison officers
- Voluntary organisations: specialist workers, project leaders
- Local people: tenants' association members.

Family groups are run by Local people who successfully complete the preparation course.

References

1. Starr, R. (1982) 'A Research Based Approach to the Prediction of Child Abuse', in Starr, R. (ed.), *Child Abuse Predictions. Policy Implications*, Ch 4. pp. 105-34, Cambridge: Ballinger publishing Co.
2. *Working Together* (1991) HMSO DoH.
3. Miller, C., Crosbie, D. and Vickery, A., (1988) *Everyday Community Care*, London NISW.

References

Part 1
The project

2 What is a family groups?

A family group is a gathering of between 8 and 12 people with their children. All are likely to live within a reasonable distance of the meeting place. The group meets once a week for 2 hours during school term-time and is led by local people who have had training in running family groups. It is financed by the initiating agencies, or through funds they have raised. It is free, or at nominal cost to the users.

The key players

Family-group workers   Local people who are recruited, prepared and selected to work in the project. They come together for support, professional advice and in-service training.

Family-group members   Men, women and children of all ages. They may be:

- People who are lonely because they are new to the area.
- People who are lonely because they have no family.
- People who have slipped through the safety net.
- People who are vulnerable but who distrust formal help.
- People who need help but who cannot be offered formal help.

Family-group workers

The group is led by a local person, and he or she is assisted by a play-group leader and an assistant play leader. They each have a contract with the funders, who may be the local authority or a voluntary agency, and a detailed job description. The group leader will have been located and trained by the project organisers, agency staff with an interest in self-help initiatives who want to work with groups and to undertake training activity. The assistance by play-group leaders assumes that the family-group membership will include young children. They will be stimulated by the play leaders whilst the adults, not all of whom will be parents, work together. Where family groups engage older persons, there may be a pair of co-leaders and no play leaders. As the involvement of parents with young children has been the most common, this guide assumes a focus on families with young children and thus the involvement of play leaders.

Family-group members

Although it is called a 'family' group, anyone can join. There is no restriction on age, sex, or ethnic origin. No one needs to state a problem to be able to join. Membership does not entail a contract to attend every week, or even to stay for a whole session. Some people may just walk in and join, others might be referred by social workers or health visitors, while others will need to be introduced personally and encouraged to stay.

It is not intended that members remain members indefinitely. The aim is to develop self-confidence, communication, self-management and other survival skills. Whilst some members are likely to become independent and no longer feel they need to attend the regular sessions, they are also likely to keep contact with the members to whom they feel closest and may return at times of particular stress. Because the focus is on local resources (human and otherwise) for local people in their locality, the family group is particularly relevant and accessible to those who otherwise would remain isolated.

Activity range

Family groups are activity based. Activities range from cooking and child-care to planning a fund-raising event. Speakers may be brought in to talk on topics such as immunisation, welfare rights or family health. It would be all too easy to suggest that having an activity focus makes setting up and running a family group simple or superficial. In practice, whilst the activities are the easiest aspect to describe, it is the interpersonal relationships, mutual support and learning, which go on within an informal context, that enhance the lives of people who might otherwise be regarded as at risk.

It is often in the discussion, which develops from the activity, or whilst the activity is going on, that the difficulties faced by members are expressed. These will range from fears about care of their children, to sadness over loss of contact with their family, to anger at partners and their circumstances. Because members are allowed to raise these issues when they feel safe and comfortable, they are more likely to listen to the response, and be able to act to change their situation, with the support available from within the group. This support may not come from the leader, but from other family group members. Members are made aware of links into, and are given knowledge about, help agencies within the locality as needs arise.

The family-group leader does not have a brief, based on a model akin to social work intervention, to intervene and change individual circumstances. The leader's task is to open up channels of help and information to formal agencies, not substitute for them. The existence of the family group can act as a preventative resource. It offers a forum for the resolution of personal and domestic stresses and problems before they escalate and require more formal interventions. For the group leader to take aside a woman who had revealed concern over her husband's possible sexual abuse of their son, and advise her beyond referring herself to social services would be stepping outside her brief. To support the woman, whilst making such a referral and dealing with the consequences, would be a role for the leader, or equally for any able and willing group member.

Aims and objectives

The agreed project aim(s) need to be clear in order to motivate both workers and members. The stated objectives — ways of achieving the aim — should be practicable and facilitate monitoring, which, in turn, will help a case for continued funding or staff time when necessary. For example:

Aim

To create a welcoming environment that attracts young parents under stress and reduces their isolation and vulnerability in the local community.

Objectives

1. To recruit an appropriate membership (recording the numbers, age, ethnic mix, etc and the apparent views of the neighbourhood if any are expressed).
2. To encourage an exchange of information, discussions and requests for guest speakers, leaflets, etc.
3. To encourage parenting skills (keeping a file of potential activities, costs, time available, etc which participants build on).

4. To encourage social skills (through, for example, running social events to help establish friendships).
5. To encourage take-up of health care (recording any increased attendance at health clinics, increased immunisation levels, etc in partnership with the members and/or health visitors as a means of monitoring the group's impact on self-care).
6. To develop self-confidence (recording activities planned by the members outside the group and recording members who move on to other things; to monitor the impact of the group on eroding isolation).

A family-group portrait

To illustrate the family group, this 'portrait' highlights a typical example of a family group in context. The nature of this example, as with all family groups, is that it reflects the needs and composition of the community in which it is located. Needs will vary from locality to locality hence the project organiser should not commence with a predetermined notion of a portrait of a family group in his or her particular locality.

A family group meets in the school building on a large council estate. The estate is unpopular. It has a high turnover of tenants. For most people, the family group is the first encounter with a group setting outside the family or work. Members' ages range from early 20s to early 60s. Half the members are single parents. Both the group leader and the play leader are women in their early 40s. Both have brought up families. The group leader has been running this group for 10 years. She received training on a preparation course.

The leaders welcome both visitors and new members tactfully and politely. Referrals to the group have been promoted by child guidance workers, health visitors, social workers, the local MP, and by an education welfare officer. The group leader has a good working relationship with all the professionals who refer members. They have the opportunity to visit the group occasionally. One member invited her own social worker to join the group.

One of those who has been referred is Jean. She has learning difficulties and is depressed — she has just moved to a new flat and is finding it difficult to adjust. Although she is still living in the area with which she is familiar, she has a new social worker and health visitor and new neighbours. Jean has one child under two whom she loves, but she has problems demonstrating any love or affection towards him. She told the group leader 'My mum did not have time or love for me . . . how could she, with eight others to look after?' Jean has a history of drug and alcohol abuse, and often she has walked the streets from early morning until late at night with her child. Jean demands a lot from the group and its leader. The leader is sensitive to this, and spends a great deal of time ensuring that other members do not dismiss Jean, but learn to understand her problems.

Group members learn to support each other, to help each other rebuild their lives and make new friendships both within the group and outside. There are discussions on a wide range of topics: budgeting on a low income, whether to shop weekly or daily, prices in different shops, basic hand sewing, using a sewing machine, making children's clothes and toys, and learning crafts such as embroidery. Activities have also centred around cooking for a children's party, and making Christmas decorations, a Christmas cake, an Advent calendar, and home-made sweets — all of which allow those on low incomes to enjoy the festivities of Christmas without yielding to the costly temptations in local shops as they previously did.

Members are informed about other activities taking place within the building. Some have taken up sewing classes and a play group leader course. For some of the members, the group might be a short-term measure until they gain the confidence necessary to move on to other activities in the community. But, for Jean and her child, the membership will be lengthy, as she continues to make friends and learn more life-skills.

3 Sample structure for family-group projects

Example 1 The single agency structure

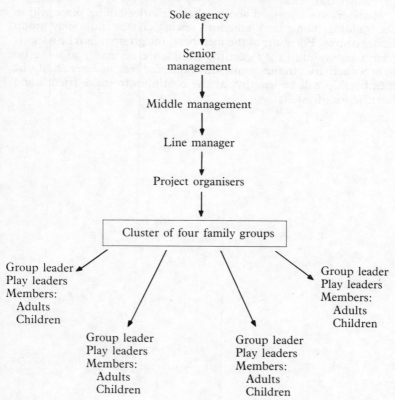

Sole agency

↓

Senior
management

↓

Middle management

↓

Line manager

↓

Project organisers

↓

Cluster of four family groups

Group leader
Play leaders
Members:
  Adults
  Children

Group leader
Play leaders
Members:
  Adults
  Children

Group leader
Play leaders
Members:
  Adults
  Children

Group leader
Play leaders
Members:
  Adults
  Children

This is the simplest structure within which to negotiate, as it is familiar to the project organisers, and will only involve a single set of procedures to access resources. However, it lacks the benefits of contrasting views and the broader resource base, which can occur where more than one agency is involved.

Example 2 Joint management committee

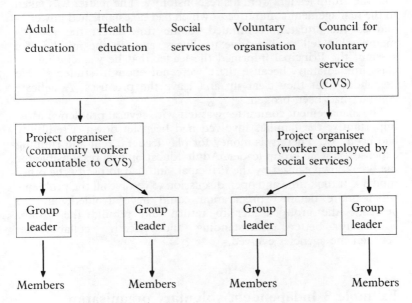

This is made up of staff from a number of agencies. The lines of accountability are extremely complex here. In one actual project based on such a structure, the funding was jointly provided by adult education, health education and social services. CVS provided administrative support, adult education paid the leader's fees, and the voluntary organisation provided a one-off cash grant. Such a structure is wide open to misunderstandings and miscommunication. The different organisations have different reasons for supporting the project. If these are not expressed openly, conflicts can arise and affect the working relationships between family-group workers funded by organisations with differing rules and expectations.

In one actual scenario, the Principal of the Adult Education Centre, responsible for the group leaders, was not comfortable with the family-group ideology. He had not been involved in the negotiations and, although his budget had been increased so that there was no loss in tutor-hours for other classes, he resented being held accountable for something he mistrusted. He began visiting one group regularly, and caused distress by referring to the members as 'deprived mothers' and 'unfortunate illiterates', and criticising activities.

The project organiser confronted the Principal, who pointed out that the group leaders were his responsibility. The matter was taken to the management committee — which had no established power — and so the situation continued. Some time later, the group's membership fell to three due to illness, and, in the middle of a session, the Principal informed the leader that he was closing the class immediately, because there were not enough 'students'. He demanded that they clear up and leave the premises. A delicate contract had been broken.

The management committee was left with several problems. Most importantly, the families involved had been let down. Credibility had been lost. There was money for play leaders, rent and running expenses, but no group leader. Adult education was responsible for the breakdown caused by the Principal, and had to pacify the other funders. It took time and open discussion to resolve all the problems which more detailed preparation could have avoided, and to persuade the group leader to return and rebuild the group. Ultimately, better understanding and effective collaboration between the agencies evolved.

Example 3 Independent voluntary organisation

This is a project, set up in its own right, consistent with the government recommended 'promotion of the independent sector'. In the actual example discussed here, the Diocesan Board of Social Responsibility and NCH funded the project in terms of staff costs and money. The local authority provided other resources and management support. To initiate such an enterprise would require a worker from one agency to cross agency boundaries and negotiate the involvement of others. The NHS and Community Care Act guidance provides the local authorities and health authorities with backing to initiate such inter-agency collaboration. Project initiators thus require a vision broader than the boundaries determined by their own agency. In this example, there were difficulties similar to those in Example 2. The project organisers were employed by different organisations, and had different conditions of service and expecta-

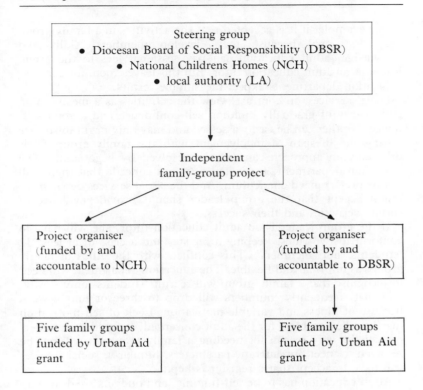

tions placed on them. This meant terms for working together had to be negotiated carefully. Accountability — to the employing bodies and to the steering group which had set up the independent voluntary organisation — needed clarification. But, once under way, the pressure of day-to-day demands forced the resolution of differences, and common ground was negotiated.

Some implications of collaboration

Family-group projects often involve the collaboration of several agencies in order to acquire adequate resources. The rules and expectations of each agency may differ and cause conflicts. Resolution of differences is essential if differences are not to undermine the work of the family groups. If the education department and social services agree to fund a group project, both must be clear about their contributions and their expectations.

For example, if it is accepted that the activities in a family group are educational because they develop members' skills and knowledge, adult education can pay sessional fees to the group leader as an adult education tutor. But this leaves room for conflict. Education departments expect measurable results.

Social services, in contrast, view the activities as a means to an end, a way of gradually building self-confidence and a good self-image. Neither can be easily assessed and may only begin to surface during the lifespan of involvement with the family group. This difference in approach can only be resolved by negotiation. The education department, for instance, might concede that there will not be pre-arranged curriculum. And the social services department might accept that the group leader should provide evidence of certain activities and their success.

If the group leader is an adult education tutor, she will have to conform to two rules: keeping a register and a class of at least 12 'students' not 'members'. This conflicts with the ethos of family groups as informal and flexible. The education department will need to recognise that a family group will recruit 'students' only slowly, and that, frequently, numbers will drop to three or four a week because of illness and variable motivation. Lack of self-motivation may be a key problem for the adult concerned. It could have under-pinned the very reason for needing a family group. It will not be resolved to meet bureaucratic parameters. Similarly, social services will have to accept that a register is kept.

Adult education has to be self-funding, and budgets are drawn up in terms of tutor-hours. Each tutor-hour is expected to bring in revenue, so membership (or class) fees are vital to the survival of an adult education or community education centre. This can create difficulties — payment of a full adult education class fee is beyond the means of most family-group members. This issue can be resolved by defining family groups as 'outreach community education' groups, a way of taking education out into the community, since the groups draw in people who would not normally take up adult education services until they have gained sufficient confidence and feel that adult education is worthwhile. Family groups thus can be seen as providing a 'taster' for a whole range of adult education classes. Using education jargon, family groups can be considered as 'access classes', for which only a nominal fee is charged, entitling 'students' to sample other classes on offer.

Alternatively, the family group can be classified as a 'special needs' class. But this can be extremely damaging — one of the major aims of a family group is to help people to shed labels and to feel like ordinary community members.

This sensitive issue is mirrored in social services. In order for resource allocation to be made easier within a social services department, a family group could be described as a 'group for isolated single parents' or 'a group for abusing parents' or 'a group for people with social disabilities'. However, such titles would make integration and acceptance by the local neighbourhood more difficult, thus destroying the purpose of family groups. Family groups should include members who have no identifiable difficulties but who wish to engage in the activities. Such labels prevent those 'more able to offer help to the less able' from identifying with the family group at all. A valuable group resource thus can be lost.

Project organisers need to acquire knowledge of how other agencies work, their needs and perceptions, and the resources they offer, in order to create an effective project structure. At the same time, they also need to understand, and be sensitive to, community politics, agendas and methods of communication, and be able to overcome suspicion and hostility by an open and honest presence in the locality.

4 Funding and costs

Funding a family-group project

Because family-group projects are not concerned with a specific client group, they often have to be funded in diverse ways. The list in Table 4.1 indicates organisations which could be approached for help and have already funded family-group projects.

Family-group projects also have been funded through grant aid: from charitable trusts, from the Commission for Racial Equality and from Urban Aid funds. In the spirit of the Griffiths Report (*NHS Community Care Act*), commercial funders such as Barclays Bank have been negotiated. The European Economic Community has also financed a preparation course. Some groups have been funded in stages, for example, at first by development monies, and could be by *Section 17(6) Children Act 1989* monies or by grant aid from voluntary bodies. Practical up-to-date information on funding sources is published regularly by the *Directory of Social Change*[1].

The family-group preparation course has its own costs which could be funded separately. The course costs which, in the model presented here, occur over 16 weeks, can be varied, as can the course structure, according to the needs of participants. Family-group preparation courses have been run on 10- and 12-week models. One course for local women was funded by Barclays Bank and ran over 10 weeks. In contrast, an ILEA-funded course, in the context of community education, ran over 32 weeks. Analysis of these variations showed that 16 weeks was the optimum/model length for best effect. The 10–12 week courses found that extra training was needed for group leaders after the groups had been set up. The lengthier courses saw a drop in motivation and a loss of focus for participants. The course is a means to an end, i.e. a family group, not just an end in itself, though it is an end in itself for some.

Whilst it is possible to ask participants to pay to attend the course,

Table 4.1.

Organisation	Can fund/contribute
Adult/community education	• Project organiser as an outreach community education worker • Family-group preparation course • Family-group leaders as adult education tutors • Free premises but not rent (but this may change with local management of schools) • Materials and equipment • Creche workers if the project is wholly an education project
Schools	• Free premises (but this may change with local management of schools) • Nursery staff where a family group has been set up in a school for children with special needs, as part of an integration programme
Health	• Creche workers • Free premises but not rent
Housing	• Project organiser as community worker • Free premises both for the family-group preparation course and family groups
Social services	• Project organisers • Family-group preparation course • Rent and free premises • Materials and equipment • Running expenses
Voluntary organisations	• As for social services

in some localities this may exclude very suitable participants. Local businesses may be prepared to fund, or make a donation towards, a course if they are acknowledged in the course literature. The course can be presented as a step towards re-introducing more people back into the job market, which will benefit businesses in the long term.

Costs

Table 4.2 outlines the actual costs of preparing the project. It is important to be aware of costs even if no actual money changes hands. Costings can contribute to a 'value for money' debate, or can be used as information for a potential independent funder.

Two project organisers (A and B) to work for 10.5 hours per week each for a period of 6 months (24 weeks): getting into the community, undertaking consultation, recruitment of course participants, setting up and designing the family-group preparation course.

Table 4.2. Family-group project preparation costs.

A = an established social worker with statutory responsibilities.	
B = a new community worker	
A = 10.5 × £x per hour × 24	= £......
B = 10.5 × £y per hour × 24	= £......
Cover time may be required on existing work of A or B so an amount may need to be allowed:	
Administrative costs of getting staff cover	= £......
To which should be added:	
Administrative costs of hiring creche workers for the course	= £......
Consultancy costs (if required)	= £......
Travel costs for visits to existing projects	= £......
TOTAL	= £......

Table 4.3. Family-group preparation course costs.

Rent: 5 hours per week for 16 weeks for two rooms (adults and creche)	= £......
Creche workers: two workers for 4 hours per week for 16 weeks	= £......
Equipment for the course and for the creche	= £......
Materials for the course and the creche	= £......
Fees for guest speakers	= £......
Transport for participants (if required)	= £ ......
Refreshment costs	= £......
Sub-total	= £......
Minus income from participants	= £ (......)
TOTAL	= £......

Once the cluster of family groups is planned, the costs can be established quite specifically. This needs to be done in advance of setting up the course, to ensure that at least a principal sum is available from funders. Table 4.4 below highlights the costs involved. These will vary according to local circumstances, for example, there may only be two family groups. In this example, the annual budget covers 20 weeks. Family groups are formed at differing frequencies which will affect the size of funds required.

Table 4.4. Family-group costs.

Four family groups: family group leaders 4 hours per week for 20 weeks	= £......
Play leaders: 3.5 hours per week for 20 weeks	= £......
Assistant play leaders: 3 hours per week for 20 weeks	= £......
Rent: 2 hours per week for 20 weeks	= £......
Running expenses: £z per week for 20 weeks	= £......
TOTAL	= £......

Paying family-group workers

Family-group workers are paid as sessional workers. The pay-scale used should be one recognised by all the funding bodies. This ensures that the project is built into the structure of the organisation responsible for it. It gives the family-group workers a sense of status and the security of knowing that their fees will be reviewed regularly, and clarifies the workers' relationship to colleagues and professional workers from other organisations. Well-drafted job descriptions should make it possible to place family-group workers on an appropriate scale. There may be problems of differentials if adult education is paying the group leader, and if another organisation is paying the assistants, e.g. play leaders on different scales. In several authorities, there is a difference of £12 between group leaders and assistants. In such cases, it can be explained that the group leader is expected to put in more than 2 hours per session. But this does make teamwork a little more difficult, and it is important to ensure that the contribution of the assistants is recognised continually and valued openly.

The amount of work the family-group workers, particularly the family-group leaders, will be expected to undertake outside the group should be taken into consideration, when deciding the rate for the job. Even though they are being paid as sessional workers, they live in the streets in which they work (this is one of the criteria for selection) and they are never off-duty, nor are they paid for sick leave or holidays.

With the inception of National Vocational Qualifications, pay may be linked to the completion of accredited courses by some agencies. Accreditation of the family-group preparation course may need consideration by the project organisers. Information on accreditation can be obtained from: National Council for Vocational Qualifications, 222 Euston Road, London NW1 2BZ.

If family-group workers are claimants at the time of appointment, loss of benefit can be prevented by calculating the annual amount of fees payable and spreading it across 52 weeks, even if it is paid monthly. (It is unlikely that the education department will be able to make these arrangements unless funding is through a grant and not as direct employment.)

There also needs to be a petty cash facility for running costs such as telephone calls, bus fares and refreshments.

Affordability

- A family-group project is affordable in that it can be tailor-made to what can be afforded and to what those involved want to achieve.
- The costs are clear and can be controlled.
- The pattern of expenditure is clear, and can be spaced flexibly and creatively over the years.
- It uses resources that are already available or under-used.
- Revenue costs can be shared creatively between collaborating agencies.

References

1. For example, *A Guide to the Major Trusts*, *A Guide to Company Giving*, *The Central Government Grants Guide*. Details of the latest editions are available from *Directory of Social Change*, Radius Works, Back Lane, London NW3 1HL.

5 Establishing an area profile

Area profiles ensure that the location of a family group is matched to local needs and identifies local people (who may become members and/or workers). The profile will be set up by the project organiser but the creation of an area profile can involve the whole team, and thus promote team-building. This process can thus be useful for all members of staff in the long term, irrespective of their ongoing role in the family-group project. It is inevitable that, by undertaking an area profile, a great deal more data will become available to the team than are needed just for the family-group project.

To obtain an area profile is a time-consuming task. Rather than focusing on gaining a picture of needs and resources just with family groups in mind, it is more cost- and time-effective to obtain a broad profile that can be drawn on for wider purposes.

The process outlined[1]

Here is a starting point for designing an area profile which can be expanded as the practice of the team develops.

1. Identify what you need to know
   (a) The population profile
       e.g. age
            sex
            race
            religious groups
   (b) The use of buildings
       e.g. commercial
            voluntary/charitable bodies, self-help and
                neighbourhood groups
            service premises, i.e. hospitals, colleges
   (c) Housing tenures
       e.g. owner-occupied
            private rented
            hostels
            council-rented
   (d) Space
       e.g. common land
            commercial land
            playspace
   (e) Travel routes
       e.g. buses
            trains

2. How did you find out?
   (a) Get copies of the small area census data relevant to your area. These can be obtained from within a local authority or direct from the Office of Public Census and will give information on housing tenure and on population.
   (b) Divide up the area into a number of streets for each worker. Each worker should then walk those streets and note the use of buildings, space and so on. Team members then meet on a pre-arranged date to pool all the information.

       Some of the resources of the area, recognised by the team as worthy of further investigation, can be marked with number stickers on a large map and referenced on a sheet attached to the map. Likewise, certain locations can be pinpointed. The map can be put on the team-room wall.

Lists can be kept of other resources not marked on the map. Some may be 'totalled' and thus indicate the degree of particular usage/need for a resource. Conclusions may be drawn: for example, a large number of estate agents may indicate something about the mobility of the population.

(c) Pool the team's knowledge of the area, both from doing (a) and (b) and from members' working knowledge of the area, identifying key agencies/individuals/voluntary organisations who may have other perspectives on the area. For example, the team may feel that local people are uncommitted to the locality. Local people might say that all the reliable bus routes lead them to the shopping area in another borough rather than to the one which is equidistant, and within the borough (where the team has been considering taking over a shopfront!).

Interview local people who have different perspectives. Some discussion of interviewing techniques may be a valuable preparation.

Interview guidance

(i) Write to the interviewee explaining your interest.

(ii) If the telephone number is available, follow up with a phone call and negotiate a time, convenient to the interviewee, to meet. This may be in the evening as many local people who act as gatekeepers of community knowledge will be in full-time employment elsewhere.

(iii) Ensure you are on time.

(iv) Explain which agency you are from, and why you want to know their views/perception of the locality. You can mention the family-group project specifically or be more global, e.g. 'My agency covers this locality and we want to know more about local people's views of services to families'.

(v) Ask if you can take notes. If s/he refuses, be prepared to write up immediately what you remember. Try to retain key words in your mind rather than word for word of what is said.

(vi) Be prepared to pass on specific issues to the relevant department/agency, for example, if the interviewer is from social services s/he may be regarded as 'part of the Council' therefore comments about the lack of lighting may be mentioned. These issues are important to the interviewee and should be respected by passing on any complaints to the Housing Department.

(vii) Be prepared to give information about yourself, your team, agency and your work in the locality. This is an opportunity to make links with key local people. Openness will help the links become strong, usable ones in the future.

(viii) If specific names of persons who may want to become members of family groups or attend the preparation courses for workers are mentioned, then check that the interviewee accepts that s/he may be referred to in the initial contact. If s/he does not wish the names to be mentioned, then ask him/her to tell the person concerned that s/he has proposed them.

(ix) Remember that the interviewee may have her/his own reasons for agreeing to meet you. Allow time for her/him to ask you questions too.

Be clear as to whether those interviewed are presenting their own views or those of their agency/group. To obtain comparable information, it is helpful to decide, as a team, which questions should be asked of the agreed list of interviewees. One team member can co-ordinate this information as the tasks are completed and try to draw up a composite of views expressed. At a later stage, this can be put to the team.

(d) As in (c), information will be obtained from the voluntary organisations/agencies interviewed, both in their roles as resources to the area and for their expressed perspectives on the locality. This information should be recorded carefully and can form the basis of an information system for the team about the area. Such a system should be integrated into the main system used by the team, thereby complementing information which may go beyond the boundaries of the area. Information collected by the team can be useful at all levels, starting from that immediately accessible and relevant to local people.

(e) The updating of information is essential in order to keep pace with the needs of the locality and keep team perspectives current. The team, on building up a profile, should decide on criteria for reviews of the information. Should these be related to staff turnover in the team? Should they be based on an agreed timescale — annually, or every election year, for example?

(f) Ultimately, the profile should consist of hard-core information on usage and population, data on resources, perspectives, plus ephemeral community gossip and other information. As a whole, it should be kept in a form which is accessible and which is possible to update without repeating the entire process.

(g) Having obtained a profile which the team feels happy with, it may be useful to hold an open event and invite local people, groups and agencies. The profile can be described from the team's perspectives. The process of designing a profile will have pointed up issues of resource gaps, needs and practice which may usefully be debated with those invited. The profile then takes on its own dynamic role in the development of practice by the team.

How to use the profile

To decide on the relevance of the family group to the locality, and to promote its existence, the area profile is the essential basis. The data must first be analyzed to identify the needs and to consolidate a picture of the resources available locally to meet them. Are there suitable premises? Is the transport route convenient for where the likely participants live? Are there local groups and activities nearby that a family group could link in to? The process of establishing an area profile can also identify possible sources of alternative or supplementary finance.

Building up a realistic picture, and checking it out with interested local people as the planning for a family group develops, is time well spent. The project organisers will need mechanisms for feeding back, in direct and positive ways, the information they have gained to both team members and to local people, keeping the family-group project to the fore. For example, one of the starting points could be a presentation by the project organisers, supported by their colleagues, to local agency workers, tenants' associations, playgroups and church groups.

The area profile in action

One community where a family-group project was at the planning stage was thought to have little local leadership and support. The agency team concerned had decided on a focus on under-fives for the project. But, after the profile was completed, the existence of an active community organisation offering a number of locally organised playgroups to young parents was identified. The team, therefore, had to decide whether to change the siting of the project, or to change the original plan and focus instead on the unexpectedly high number of isolated elderly people shown by the profile.

In another team, experienced workers repeatedly insisted that 'We don't have any ethnic minority groups here'. This usually means that there have not been any referrals, rather than that there is no ethnic minority presence. One social worker, in particular, was adamant that there were no Asians in the area, even when it was pointed out that there was a Mosque in the same street as the social services office. Judgements about localities must be made on the basis of data gained through area profiling, not on individual personal perceptions.

References

1.   Hearn, B., and Thomson, B. (1987) *Developing Community Social Work in Teams: A Manual for Practice*, pp. 44—45. London: NISW.

6 Building the infrastructure

The key dimensions of a family-group project

The key dimensions of a family-group project are: setting up the infrastructure, training family group leaders, and finally setting up the family groups. Building the infrastructure requires obtaining staff, finance and material resources, and locating the sites for the family groups. This overlaps with preparing the training course for the local people who will become family-group leaders. A scheme is illustrated in Fig. 6.1.

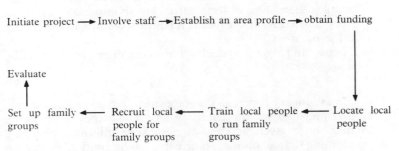

Fig. 6.1. Setting up a family-group project.

The product of this process is a cluster of family groups within a locality, and requires the involvement of all levels of staff, and of a wide range of local people. Commitment, adequate patience and good timing are essential. Getting under way requires initially that someone recognises the need to act, to de-isolate vulnerable people, thereby reducing the risks to well being that isolation brings. It is important that time is given to the initial stages of a project, as a great deal of credibility will be lost if a family group is publicised locally and then folds because the resources are not released as anticipated.

Action summary

1. Clarify and agree the aims and objectives of the project.
2. Collectively, create a profile of the neighbourhood in which the project is to be set up.
3. Review the aims and objectives of the project in the light of the new information.
4. Review resources available, and possibly make new decisions about who should be the project organisers.
5. Draw up and agree a project schedule detailing all the major events, such as: further discussion with local people, recruitment of potential course participants, starting up the family-group preparation course.
6. Discuss and agree staff cover: dates and days when it will be available.
7. Discuss and agree administrative resources, and when they need to be available.
8. Discuss and agree how, and when, the project organisers will keep their 'home' team involved in the project. (Guest speakers are needed on the family-group preparation course, and there is no reason why a colleague or colleagues should not be amongst them. End-of-term parties are an important feature of every course and colleagues can be invited along to contribute to the occasion.)
9. Discuss and agree a method of monitoring and reporting progress.

The action summary covers all the stages necessary to ensure that the ground is prepared for the family group. The stages need not be taken in the order given, and who carries responsibility for what may vary according to local norms. Some parts can be omitted depending upon the circumstances of the initiating worker and of the triggering agency. When the initiative comes from main-grade staff, or from local people themselves, the entire process probably will be appropriate if local authority resources and support are seen to be crucial. However, if there is a political initiative, then senior level commitment may exist already. Equally, if family groups are already in existence elsewhere within the authority's boundaries, or within those of the key voluntary agency in the area, the preparation may be relatively speedy. Here a 'greenfield' site, where all persons are new to the notion, is assumed.

The key players in setting up a project

Project initiators People who are seized by the idea and who persuade others to consider setting up a project.

Managers at all levels They secure the goodwill that releases resources: time, people, money.

Project organisers Two professional members of staff who work together as project organisers. They recruit, prepare, select and support the local people. They liaise with other professional workers.

Project initiators

The initiator needs to have good negotiating and persuading skills. The initiator eventually may become an organiser or may identify who will be. The time required to set the project in motion will depend upon local conditions and upon the desire of the initiator to keep pushing the project forward. But, it is important that preparations are undertaken thoroughly, in order to ensure that the philosophy of a family-group project is adopted by all those involved, either directly or indirectly. At any point, the project initiator may engage other workers and/or local people to assist in this preparation. Local circumstances will dictate the appropriate mix.

The initiator's role entails:

1. Gaining agreement — often at committee level in a local authority — that the project will fit in with current policies and strategies. Funding for a minimum of 3 years is the target, although economic conditions may force year-on-year funding. This, of course, would be time-consuming and would diminish the focus on the groups themselves. Also, it may lengthen the active involvement of the initiator who otherwise might expect to withdraw. If more than one department or organisation is concerned, then the project will need to be justified from a number of different perspectives. The reason for an education department agreeing to participate will be quite different from that of the social services or a health or a voluntary organisation, for example.

2. Obtaining a decision at middle-management level on the general location of the project within the organisation, and confirmation of the staff who are taking responsibility for setting up the family group. If staff are involved from more than one organisation, lines of accountability, and procedures for joint working, will have to be set up and agreed by all.
3. Convincing other staff not directly involved that the project is of value to them and to the community they serve, and that the availability and allocation of resources has been thought through.
4. Identifying who should be the key workers setting up the project (project organisers), and how their time is going to be used. The process of identifying can be used to build a team commitment to, and ownership of, the project.
5. Preparing and planning a project schedule so that resources can be made available at the right time, and so that the project organiser's time can be released.

When the initiating agency is a local authority, elected members may be involved. They may initiate action from their positions as local people. Their involvement may be due also to the financial elements in the decision to pursue a family-group project.

Managers

The senior manager's role in a non-decentralised agency may entail:

1. Defining the objectives of the project, and clarifying how they will benefit the organisation's overall policies.
2. Considering whether the project is a single pilot scheme, or whether it is more cost and time-effective to set up several simultaneously.
3. Drawing up a three-year staffing and budget plan.
4. Planning collaborative funding options with other organisations which could be involved.
5. Acquiring the resources from existing budgets, or through negotiation with elected members.
6. Working out, with middle and line managers, the most appropriate area(s) for the project(s) to be sited.
7. Resolving employment issues, concerning local people, before the project organisers start to recruit course participants and design the course.

Middle managers will have to decide which team would be best placed to develop the project, and in which area it would best be located.

Line managers will have to consider the resources in the team —
who might enjoy the work, for instance, and how many staff could
be released. The middle manager and the line manager will explore
how the nomination of the project organisers might further management objectives, spread the cost of the project across several
budgets, enable staff to be relieved from excessive stress, and help
expand the repertoire of interventions offered by the team to
families.

Project organisers

Project organisers are likely to be agency workers who have the task
of developing the project for 6 months. In the preparatory phase,
project organisers, particularly if part-timers, may need to negotiate
overtime options with their employer. This can be budgeted for in
terms of the overall project costs. It is they who will consult with
local groups, individuals, agency workers who may know people in
need of support and engage their interest. Their most valuable
resource is the team's area profile and their own knowledge of the
area. Protocol needs to be observed. For example, the line manager
may have to write to agency workers in a similar line management
position to inform them about the project, and to ask for permission
for the project organisers to meet their staff.

The organisers need to:

1. Be clear about why the project is necessary and how it will fit
   into the organisation's policies, or how it might strengthen
   policies in other departments.
2. Consult with everyone who might be affected by the setting-up
   of the project, and develop common understanding, trust and
   acceptance among likely users, workers, agency staff and local
   people.
3. Set up a course to equip local people to facilitate the group,
   creating a structure for people to work together.
4. Assess and advise course participants on their suitability for
   family-group work, make recommendations to the future
   funders, and help the family-group workers appointed to set up
   their groups.
5. Provide the family-group workers with agency staff support,
   both in a group setting, and on a one-to-one basis, as local
   people will need access to agency services and help at times.
6. Provide training on issues, as they arise, for the family group
   workers, after the basic training.

Locating the project organisers: two examples

1. A team, which was very keen to develop a project, had the highest intake in the social services area and the highest under-fives population. But it was short of a Grade III social worker. One of the two social workers responsible for child protection was an excellent case worker and nearing retirement. She was fairly sceptical about the family-group project. The second social worker was showing signs of stress and needed a chance to work more positively. However, social services for elderly people were not over-stretched. One family aide had great potential for development but could not, at that time, be seconded on to a Certificate in Social Service course.

   The workers had a friendly, supportive relationship. The line and middle managers proposed to senior management that monies not being used for the third statutory case worker should be used to buy in cover for the second social worker. This would not increase the establishment figures, and new money would not have to be found. The family aide was nominated as the other project organiser. Cover time was not needed for her and, as her salary came out of a different budget, this meant the line manager was able to spread the cost, and offer two members of staff professional and personal opportunities to learn a new way of working.

2. A social services department recently had been restructured and was 'going local'. The residential services were also being encouraged to become community orientated. In one area, there was considerable coolness between the social work team and the residential home for handicapped children. This was more through lack of a daily working partnership than through any real animosity. The middle manager and line manager decided to nominate a social worker and the supervisor of the residential home as project organisers. Not only did they have complementary skills but the residential supervisor was able to get into the community, making contacts relevant to the residential home and learning community development skills appropriate to community care. Again, the staffing costs were spread over two budgets.

7 Managing the project

Core tasks for project organisers

Setting up the project involves the following practical tasks for organisers:

1. To make contact in the neighbourhood with professionals, local groups, local leaders and local people. To record addresses of those interested in the project, and details of any resources on offer.
2. To gather at least 30 names of potential course participants (to become family-group leaders). To record sources of names, known connections between people, and to record which people, if any, have been already seen by the project initiators.
3. To recruit 20 local people on to the family-group preparation course — to check police records if there is a policy to do so. To record addresses, telephone numbers, relevant experience and skills.
4. To plan the family-group preparation course. To prepare the course programme, taking into account timing suitable to participants and the need for creche facilities.
5. To tutor a course that produces the required number of family-group workers able, and willing, to set up the family groups. To record whether the course participants stay, whether they apply for posts, and whether they have shown the potential to be consistent, available and approachable.
6. To arrange interviewing and appointment of the family-group workers. To ensure the funding agency's finance and conditions are confirmed.
7. To set up the family groups with the family-group leaders. To make arrangements for providing continuing support.

Sharing responsibilities

Carrying out these tasks entails attending to the related management procedures. It is important that the line manager keeps in close touch with the project because there will be many administrative matters that the project organisers will not be authorised to deal with, and it is up to the line manager to be sure that these are actually dealt with, and on time (see Table 7.1).

Table 7.1.

Procedure	Responsibility
• Ensure that there is cover time	Line manager
• Use the cover time that has been provided	Project organisers
• Ensure that there is administrative back up	Line manager
• Agree a timetable of meetings within the project for support and supervision	Line manager and project organisers
• Draft job descriptions for family-group workers which comply with the aims and objectives of the project	Project organisers
• Agree job descriptions with the team	Line manager and project organisers
• Ensure that the job descriptions are correctly graded and processed into the system	Line manager
• Ensure that procedures are set up for paying the family-group workers, and for paying the running expenses in advance	Line manager
• Make arrangements for the payment of rent for premises the project will use	Line manager
• Ensure that decisions are taken about police and medical checks	Line manager
• Check out any insurance issues and ensure that there is correct cover	Line manager
• Draft a letter of employment for the family-group workers	Line manager and project organisers
• Ensure that the letter and the conditions laid out in it are approved and confirmed at a senior level and in all the appropriate departments	Line manager
• Write a brief for the creche workers	Project organisers

Table 7.1 continued

Procedure	Responsibility
• Ensure that creche workers are employed. This may involve internal and external advertising and formal interviews	Line manager
• Discuss how job applications and interviews for the course participants wishing to become family-group workers are to be handled	Line manager and project organisers
• Assist project organisers in consulting with the community by liaising with fellow managers in other agencies	Line manager and senior management
• Undertake the appointment of the family-group workers and confirm appointments	Line manager and project organisers

Inter-team and interagency working

The allocation of the responsibilities is relatively easy if the project organisers have the same line manager. However, a single agency may decide to set up two projects in two different areas, nominating a project organiser from each area, and expecting the two nominees to work as a team. The pressures and timetables in the two teams concerned may be quite different and inhibit the two project organisers from working together effectively. It will then have to be decided at a senior level whether there should be a co-ordinator to liaise with the two managers, or whether one of the managers should assume a management role for both of the project organisers.

If two separate agencies collaborate to set up a family-group project, the potential difficulties become more complicated. If adult education is providing one project organiser, for example, this organiser's week will be arranged quite differently from that of a community worker in a voluntary organisation, or of a social worker in a local authority. In addition, if adult education is funding the group leaders, job descriptions become an issue. Adult education will need to write the job descriptions in a completely different way, emphasising only the 'educational' tasks and not the 'caring' tasks.

Any line manager or project organiser taking on a mixed funding family-group project should be as confident as possible that senior management of both agencies have addressed the issues of: how the project is to be managed, how accountability is to be implemented, and that the funding issues have been properly resolved.

8 Scheduling supervision for project organisers

Supervision of the family-group projects will be required by those involved at different points in the process.

Project organisers

Initially, it will be through an existing supervisory framework that project organisers are likely to be identified. The supervision of staff members is likely to include areas of professional development and an awareness of matching these to organisational goals. The supervision session will make it possible to highlight the strengths and areas for growth of a worker. Through such analysis, the suitability of a staff member to act as a project organiser will become evident.

Where project organisers come from different teams of even from different agencies, it may become an issue as to who acts as supervisor to the project organisers. If one agency has an established history of staff supervision when the partnering agency does not, difficulties may arise. The identified supervisor may need to be prepared to negotiate supervision time with the line manager in the partnering agency. In addition, that supervisor may have to be prepared to give the supervision to both project organisers, even when one is from another agency. The worker who does not normally have supervision may become seduced or irritated by the process. It is important, therefore, to set all the parameters clearly and in advance of commencement. Any differences of view or expectation then can be negotiated openly.

Where there are two project organisers, and two supervisors, it is expedient and efficient to agree that one supervisor takes responsibility. This should be decided according to the knowledge base, expertise and willingness of the supervisors to be committed to the project.

The critical points

Once the location of the project has been agreed, the project organisers will then move on to establishing the family-group worker preparation course. At this time, most project organisers are being asked to perform tasks outside their professional training. This can be daunting. It is therefore essential that supervision sessions are held at the critical points of the project for the organisers. These are:

1. The point at which the project organisers are starting to go out into the community to locate potential family-group workers and design the course for them.
2. Six weeks later, or half-way through the consultations with local people about the recruitment process for the course.
3. Six weeks later, when the consultation and recruitment has been completed, and the family-group preparation course is about a month off.
4. Half-way through the course.
5. Three weeks before the end of the course.
6. When the course has finished, and appointments have been made.
7. When the groups are being set up.

First supervision

This supervision should make sure that the project organisers have the information and support which they need to start their job. The project plan and deadlines should be re-confirmed.

Possible questions

- Has adequate time been allowed?
- Have the job descriptions been drafted and sent on to the appropriate people?
- Are administrative resources satisfactory?
- Has transport been arranged and costed?
- Have all community contacts been alerted?
- How are the project organisers planning to use their time?
- Which contracts are their priorities? Why?
- Have they allocated a period to plan and design the family-group preparation course?

- What procedures have they decided to follow if a potential participant is recommended?
- Have they produced any leaflet-style publicity?

Second supervision

This should ensure that the agreed tasks have been completed. By this stage, the project organisers should have collected at least 20 – 25 names. It is important to find out who suggested the names of the potential participants. For instance, if more than two or three people have been recommended by an organisation such as a single parents' club or a bereavement counselling service, their agenda could take over the preparation course.

Similarly, a professional worker could be using the group as a way of diverting awkward customers. And, if three or four participants have been recruited from the ranks of child-minders, foster parents and other volunteers already known to the organisation, then the project is failing to reach out to the community. There is also a danger that colleagues are seeing the preparation course as a substitute for training which they are not able to provide. This, again, could skew the preparation course.

At this stage, management tasks such as job descriptions and payment need to be resolved. The first draft of the preparation course needs to be considered, making sure that it is a genuine attempt to look at life from the perspective of an ordinary person, and that it strengthens the aims and objectives of the project. The course should not make extensive use of guest speakers. The project organisers are not expected to be expert tutors and should not call in experts to cover their own inexpertise. Their role is the same as that of the family-group workers: drawing out other people's knowledge and skills, and bringing in the experts only when unavoidable.

Possible questions

- What is the schedule for visiting potential course participants at home?
- When do the project organisers plan to select the course participants, and how will people be notified?
- Do they have any other opportunities to offer people who have not been selected on to the course?

Third supervision

The purpose of this session is to talk through the selection of the course participants, examining ages, life experience, circumstances and ethnic mix. The process of selection can be quite tough for the project organisers and they will need support. It might be reassuring for the project organisers to spend a day with someone who has already run a family-group preparation course.

Fourth supervision

By now, the project organisers will probably be confident and enjoying the course as much as the participants, but there could be problems. For example, a dominant person or clique may be causing conflict. Talking about these difficulties is important, in order to prevent the project organisers feeling demoralised or unable to cope. Project organisers will need to talk through their anxieties about making recommendations, and about advising those who need professional counselling not to apply.

Fifth supervision

The course is almost over. It is time for a review, most specifically about the recommendation process, and the project organisers need to de-brief. Arrangements will have to be clarified for participants to make applications and for short-listing and interviews. Decisions may have to be taken about whether the full quota of groups will be set up or not.

Sixth supervision

Once the appointment of the family-group workers has been completed, there will be administrative matters to sort out. It will also be important to deal sensitively with the disappointed applicants, in order to avoid further difficulties when the groups are being set up. There will need to be a formal review, and possibly a report for senior managers and/or the funding body(ies).

Seventh session

This is a difficult time for everyone. The project organisers will have to make a final assessment. They will need support from their supervisor and team, particularly if a wrong selection has been made, and if changes have to be negotiated.

During these sessions, the supervisor should also allow space for organisers to express their feelings, particularly their anxieties. The project will put the organisers, who will have other work to do as well, under stress. This is particularly so with workers who have limited experience in training and working with groups. As the organisers move upward along their own learning curve, the supervisor has to both challenge and support. The supervisor may need to challenge on issues such as the racial mix of the group, the plans for cross-fertilisation between groups, assumptions about women's roles and the inclusion of men. They need to support out frustrated plans, elusive time-scales and air their own criticism of the approach of the organisers. The supervisor has to be committed to the project but retain objectivity in relation to the process as well.

Group leaders

Most project organisers are unskilled in 'staff supervision' and can revert quickly to treating the group leaders as clients. Moreover, the leaders are not staff, so support and a continuation of the ethos of personal growth established in the preparation course is not only more appropriate for local people but also more consistent with the project philosophy than is formal supervision.

The keys are:

1. The group workers are supported through their peer group which meets monthly (this works out about three times a term — nine times a year for costing purposes).
2. It is not advisable to hold the meetings in anyone's home — this sets up a whole range of inappropriate peer-group dynamics.
3. The project organiser performs the three functions described below.

Administrative ensuring a room is booked, warm/cool, clean, and that the leaders are notified if there are any changes, ensuring that refreshments are available.

handing out pay cheques, and petty cash, auditing the petty cash books and collecting pay claims and leaders reports.

Enabling continuing the process, started on the preparation course, of enabling the leaders to develop their own community leadership network/support group.

ensuring that the play leaders play a full part in the peer group and do not become second-class citizens. This can happen very easily because of the pay differential. But, remember that the children are full members of the family group, their development needs must always be kept on par with those of the adults. Failure to support play leaders in this way can result in a rapid turnover of play leaders and consequential disturbance to the children.

Facilitating lines of communication and feed-back between the leaders and formal agencies. Common concerns, issues and information, will come out in the peer-group discussion which are of value to a range of agencies. For example: bad attitude and behaviour of a GP's receptionist; the moving-in of a family under stress; who may be moonlighting and whose files are unlikely to have come with them. The project organiser will have to agree with the leaders the best way of handling such material.

identification of training and development needs of the leaders, and making sure they are met.

By undertaking those three functions sensitively, and with eyes wide open, the project organiser can support, monitor and evaluate the progress of each leader, and each group, without undermining their role as independent community leaders.

For example: a petty cash book may reveal that macramé materials have been bought 6 weeks in a row. This would mean that the leader has run out of ideas, or that one person is dominating the group and is proving hard to interest in anything else without causing total disruption; or that everyone is working like mad to produce macrame hangers for the stall at the fete to raise money for the summer outing.

Skilful facilitating of issues such as new ideas, difficult people or fund-raising within the peer group prevents a person's self-confidence from being undermined, and produces a range of experience, advice and ideas that is not possible in one-to-one supervision. It also strengthens the leader's peer group.

The leaders need to know a phone number and time when the project organiser is available, and to be confident that, if they are not there, messages will be passed on quickly and reliably.

Some one-to-one support may be necessary on a practical level at the beginning. For example, dealing with an awkward caretaker, or transporting toys. But this should rapidly tail off and one-to-one counselling/support should be actively discouraged.

Termly visits to the groups is important and usually valued by the leaders. But, they should be done always by prior arrangement with the leader. The very first visit should be towards the end of the first term, unless the tender specifically requires otherwise, in which case the reasons have to be thoroughly understood.

It should also be made clear to colleagues that they must make arrangements with the leaders before they visit the groups.

Part 2
The project
preparation course

Preparation course

The course in this Manual concentrates on family life and on young children. The focus can be changed according to local needs, for example, focusing on special learning needs and substituting information about this in the sessions devoted to child development. Similar substitution can be made if you are developing 'care for the carer's group', focusing on elderly people, or those with mental health problems. The essential thing is to retain the ethos of the course which is that of working from where the local people are, at the point of commencement.

9 Recruiting course participants

Co-operating with local people

In a family-group project, the project organisers are not in authority, but are seeking permission, through a process of consultation, to work in co-operation with people who live in the neighbourhood. These are the experts on neighbourhood life, the organisers are not. Such co-operation must be based on open partnership, with duties and responsibilities clearly spelt out on both sides. Once local people accept that the project is a co-operative venture, and that the organiser can offer a preparation course and possibly a sessional job, the process will become easier.

Going into a neighbourhood, and finding partners to work with, can be a daunting prospect. There are no prescribed methods for this because it is a process of building relationships, and each party will have individual perceptions, gifts and needs. The final phase — setting up of the family groups — depends on referrals from agencies, from families themselves, and from the promotional work undertaken by the family-group leader and project organiser. If thorough attention has been paid to designing the infrastructure and the process of recruiting course participants, it is likely that a list of potential family-group members will have evolved ready for opening the family groups, or that active contacts will be ready with names once the start date is identified.

The process of finding course participants enables project organisers to meet and enthuse other people who might be interested in family groups. A headteacher will know of parents who are active in supporting the school, and who may work in a family group; there may be space available in the school for a family group. The co-operation of the caretaker could be sought, and s/he may know

dinner staff who, in turn, will probably know of people in the
neighbourhood who might be interested in the course (see Table
9.1).

Table 9.1. Possible contacts who could advise on potential course participants

Social Services neighbourhood/area office
- Social workers
- Home-helps
- Family aides
- Under-eights officers
- Community workers
- Fostering officers
- Intermediate treatment workers

Adult education centre
- Community education outreach workers
- Special needs tutors
- Literacy and numeracy tutors
- Home economics tutors

Health clinics and well-women clinics
- Health visitors
- Community health workers
- Counsellors

Doctors' surgeries
- Doctors
- Receptionists
- Health visitors
- Nursing staff
- Counsellors

Schools
- Headteachers
- Teachers
- Caretakers
- Dinner staff
- Lollipop ladies

Local centres
- Welfare rights centres
- Community relations councils
- Councils of voluntary service (for lists of local organisations)
- Law centres
- Libraries
- Volunteer bureaux
- Civic centre (for lists of local organisations and groups)
- Local authority community centres
- Youth centres

Table 9.1 continued

Community health
- Community mental handicap teams
- Community psychiatric social workers
- Community nurses
- District nurses

Local contact points
- Religious leaders (including minority groups)
- Parent and toddler groups
- Play-group leaders
- Shopkeepers
- Community centres/youth clubs/social clubs
- Tenants' associations
- Carers
- Volunteer/befrienders

Will the neighbourhood 'buy' the project idea? Project organisers must take time to think through the concerns, perceptions and roles of the individuals or groups that they are going to meet with in order to discuss the project. It may be, for example, that a health visitor is very concerned about depression amongst parents and the lack of preventive health-care take-up. The headteacher may be concerned about school non-attendance and lack of communication with a group of parents, which the health visitor has also identified. The health visitor will be interested in the health education and self health-care that takes place in a family group. The headteacher will be interested in the adult education element of family groups and with the opportunities parents will have to learn about the education process, and how they may be involved in their children's education.

Local groups, run by local people, will have other agendas and sensitivities. For example, a parent and toddler group will be sensitive about the service they are offering being duplicated. They may be angry that financial resources which have been denied to them are being given to the project. But the organisers' goodwill will be a key factor in recruiting potential course participants, and in local people accepting family groups into the network of neighbourhood resources.

Recruitment preliminaries

Organisers should have a clear profile of the skills and personal qualities required for the family-group workers. These may be warmth, a sense of humour, ability to listen and understand other people, budgeting skills and reliability. There may be specific requirements related to the project, like knowledge of child development or fluency in a particular language. From the outset, project organisers need to be clear about what is going to be expected from the group leader, play leader and assistant play leader.

Course participants should be recruited from the area where the groups are going to be set up. If the plan is to set up four groups in four different localities, there needs to be a minimum of eight people from each locality, in order to allow for drop-out, self-selection-out, and the organisers' own selection processes.

Premises for the family-group preparation course must be identified. Who controls premises, and the stigma attached to some venues, will need to be considered. Some local people who control premises may feel their authority threatened. For example, a community centre caretaker may exercise great control over the centre's use. Through negotiation with the tenants' association, the resistant caretaker may be side-stepped by project organisers in order to hold a course at the centre. On some estates, negotiating skills and knowledge of systems have been used deliberately to make centres and rooms available to a wider number of local people who have previously been denied access by the local 'mafia'. In addition to making local contacts, organisers should also arrange for the preparation course to be advertised, in order to draw on as wide a field as possible. Any advertisements have to be precise about the locality and about any other requirements that will be expected of the course participants.

Letters

Letters are the best way to make first contact, although there may be no response. The letter should be addressed to the relevant person, should outline the project organiser's role and should be followed up with a telephone call. A standard letter can be prepared to be sent to the potential contacts/course participants. This should include:

1. The name of the person who suggested the potential contact/recruit.
2. The project organisers' name and telephone number.
3. Days, dates and times when the organiser can visit.
4. Days, dates and times when the organiser can be contacted.
5. The deadline for contact to be made with the organiser for consultation to take place.
6. Some information and background on the project.

If leaflets are prepared, words like isolated, vulnerable, poor, inadequate must be avoided scrupulously, as they are hurtful and misleading. The project is about providing the opportunity to share skills and information, to make friends and hopefully to 'have a laugh'. Protocol must always be observed rigorously in approaching local professional workers, local groups, or individuals, especially when asking for help from minority groups whose sense of isolation and alienation is increased by insensitivity.

Meetings with local groups

Any meetings should be set up either on the group's own territory or on neutral territory. The organiser must listen to both what is being said and what is not said. A time limit should be set and adhered to — all concerned are busy people. The organiser should never 'talk down', but, at the same time, should try to avoid professional jargon. The language used will reveal how the organiser really perceives the project, and this will be picked up by local people.

It may be necessary to change the location of the project, or to revise aims and objectives to meet the previously unidentified needs of the local people in the neighbourhood. This may have funding implications. For example, funding agreed through *Section 17 Children Act 1989* cannot be issued by a local authority for a project focusing on elderly people.

The organiser must be prepared, at meetings, to go through the different stages of consultation sensitively, and at an appropriate pace, to answer questions, and record names only with agreement. The organiser must always be clear about which point has been reached during the meeting, and to have the correct information available.

Home consultation/interview

The home setting is the ideal location for interviewing prospective participants, but many project organisers are anxious about a home consultation and try to find ways of avoiding it. A home consultation shows that the prospective participant's time is valued, that the organiser is willing to travel to them rather than vice versa. People are more relaxed at home. However, the organiser is visiting as a guest, and should behave accordingly. This entails being aware of the cultural values of the home visited. For example, four visits may well be necessary when recruiting women from the Asian community; first to meet the woman herself, then her husband, then her mother-in-law, and finally the grandmother-in-law who will decide whether the course is suitable, and whether the organiser is respectable.

If people living in the neighbourhood are thinking of becoming involved in the project, issues of confidentiality and responsible behaviour will be of paramount importance to them. Project organisers need to be honest about what they can, and cannot, achieve, and value all the information that is shared with them, however unimportant or flawed it may appear. It is part of the jigsaw the organiser is piecing together. A family-group project is anchored by consulting at every stage.

When interviewing prospective participants, organisers should make sure that they:

(a) have time for and commitment to the course.
(b) know the courses are free but that there are costs for the participants to consider: bus fares, creche costs, etc.
(c) understand the purpose of the course including the fact that it may not lead to paid employment, but will be enjoyable and useful in its own right.

The organiser should then assess the interviewee's perception of a 'course'. Have they, for example, attended and completed courses before? Why did they do them, and what is their view of them now?

The organiser needs to tell prospective participants:

- why they are being approached.
- what the project is.
- what family groups are.
- how formal the course is.
- how much reading and writing is required.
- how long the course is, dates and times, and what it is about.
- where it is and how they can get there.
- what creche facilities there are.
- whether they will be expected to stay to lunch, what facilities there are and what the arrangements are going to be.
- what other facilities are nearby, e.g. shops, cafes, etc.
- whether there is an exam.
- whether they get an attendance certificate.
- whether there is a job.

It is unwise to tell an interviewee there and then that they are being accepted on the course. It is necessary to review all the people interviewed to get the correct balance of skills, qualities and age mix, and this should be explained at the interview. It is also important for the interviewee to have time to reflect and discuss the course and project with others. But, the organiser must tell the interviewee when they will be contacted. This must be in good time for them to make any necessary domestic arrangements.

There may be people who are very keen but totally unsuitable. It is fairest to counsel them away from the course at the interview, and to have alternatives to offer them. In the process of getting into the community, the organiser will learn about other courses, groups and activities. It may be that the person interviewed has very heavy commitments at home which precludes her/him joining the course, but is extremely lonely. It may be possible to arrange for her/him to be visited by a member of a local carer's group. Alternatively, the interviewee may be a young parent who would benefit more from the Pre-School Play Group Association Foundation Course.

Essential resources

On the surface, these tasks look simple, but they are hard work and the following resources are essential:

1. Time — a minimum of one-and-a-half days for each organiser: one day each working on the streets and half a day together, to review what has been achieved, and to plan how to spend the next preparation day in the following week.
2. The support of the agency team and other colleagues. It will be necessary to feed back useful information to the team on a regular basis to keep up their interest, and avoid resentment from office-bound colleagues.
3. A pair of comfortable shoes!
4. Regular meetings with a supervisor. It is easy to get too close to a project, or to feel that some problem is insurmountable. The organiser will need an outsider with whom to talk through ideas and express frustrations.

10 Pre-course practicalities

Resource review

Before going further in preparing the project, it is valuable to review the resources in the light of the area profile and any changed circumstance within the team. Financial resources can often be the most elusive, particularly if an agency's own funding changes, for example, through community charge capping. A budget may have to be agreed in principle, but, until the line manager knows what resources are actually secured, a final budget cannot be drawn up. The cost of rent for premises, the cost of the project organiser's time, whether funds are located under the same or under different budget heads all will need to be checked. The availability of premises should also be confirmed, in case another group has purchased space during the profiling period. The availability of transport will need to be checked if the area profile suggests it may be needed.

Resentment can quickly grow within the initiating team if staff feel that the project is eating up a disproportionate amount of time, dictating duty rotas, influencing the allocation of cases, and calling upon administrative time and resources. Unless the whole team is involved and kept informed, the sense of common ownership is lost and the benefits of developing a community-based project are not experienced by everyone. At worst, the 'people' resource could be withdrawn.

The budget should now be available for creche workers' sessional fees, speakers' fees and rent for the rooms used (unless owned by the agency). Administrative arrangements for paying creche workers' fees should be clarified. Some petty cash may be needed for unexpected costs, such as nappies. The responsibility for ensuring training material is ready, and equipment available for the course and creche lies with the project organiser.

Premises need to be available for 16 weeks and be accessible by local transport. There will have to be both a room for the course and another for the creche. Premises must be well heated. The owner-ship of the premises may be relevant, depending on the local politics identified during the area profiling stage. The number of creche workers will depend on the number and age of the children of participants on the course. But, there should be one qualified worker, possibly two, and an assistant. They will be needed for 16 weeks, 1 day a week for 4 hours — 2 hours in the morning and 2 hours in the afternoon. They should be employed well in advance. The under-eights section in the local authority will advise about the relevant regulations. Creche workers will need to be briefed about the objectives of the course, and what is expected of them, and any difficulties will need to be clarified.

Who are the participants?

Throughout this guide, the word 'participant' is deliberately used in relation to those on the course to convey the fact that people will be expected to participate, to contribute as equals, and to be democratically in control of the course. When project organisers have consistently referred to the people on the course as 'members' the people have behaved liked members, having needs met, and not as equal responsible adults.

The family-group preparation course may be the first course a participant has ever attended. Or, it may be the first contact with people with legally enforceable powers. This may lead to reticence, curiosity, or fear on the part of the participant. Thus, it is important to establish a welcoming and open style, where questions are encouraged. Bad planning, or lack of communication between the project organisers, will be picked up quickly by the participants and will devalue the course in their eyes.

If participants are recruited from a multicultural community, days of religious observance must be taken into account when deciding which day to hold the course (see Table 10.1 below). Similarly, including a course session on friendship, although impor-tant, is not necessarily the best vehicle for exploring confidentiality in a culture which works through the extended family rather than through friendship networks.

Family-group work is not about crisis intervention but about prevention. So, the course is not about training people who already have a professional training, or trying to create mini-professionals.

Instead, the course should draw out and develop the everyday caring skills that people have acquired already through everyday living. Accordingly, the time needed to prepare the course must not be underestimated. The content (which must relate to the aims and objectives of the project), the training materials, the pacing of the course, and the degree of flexibility, must all be discussed by the organisers. The course programme has to be agreed, responsibilities allocated, training material prepared, guest speakers briefed, creche workers employed and briefed, and the venue arranged.

Time scheduling

The development of the time schedule is one of the most complex and sensitive tasks the staff group will have to undertake in creating a project in partnership with local people. There needs to be a timetable for planning meetings and management meetings, with a chart showing the personal commitment of staff for the next 18 months. (Once the project is under way, the project organisers will not be able to take holiday leave, or to go on training courses.) A second chart will be necessary to show the school and religious holidays relevant to the local community (see Table 10.1).

Professionals often make the mistake of trying to make ordinary people's timetables fit theirs. This can be illustrated by one actual example. A social worker was trying to enlist the help of local parent and toddler groups in the prevention and early detection of child neglect. The local-group organisers were enthusiastic, and eager to co-operate and undergo some training. The social worker arranged training at a 'suitable' time, 17.00 – 19.00, just between the end of office work and the beginning of evening meetings. But, at this time, the local people were busy welcoming partners, feeding their families, and putting small children to bed. So the plan was revised to compress three evenings' training into one day. The day chosen by the social worker was during the school half-term — with no creche facility or plan for keeping older children amused.

The third attempt took these lessons into account, but the social worker's invitation now met with little response. The failure to take local people's responsibilities and needs into account had confirmed the group organiser's fears: that they were being treated as an extension of social services and would be used as 'spies'. Eventually, however, they were won over by the promise of a code of practice.

Table 10.1. Local and professional key events chart

Month	Local people	Professional workers
January	• Greek/Coptic Orthodox Christmas. Hindu religious festival. Recovering from Christmas. Poor health in families usual. Bad weather for taking out small children. School term begins.	
February	• Poor weather/poor health continues. School half-term.	
March	• Easter. The Night of the Journey and Ascension — Muslim festivals. Mahashivrati — Hindu festival. School holidays.	Complete annual leave
April	• Ramadan (30 days) begins — Muslim festival. Baisakli — Sikh festival. Ramavmi — Hindu festival Days of Pesach — Jewish festival. School holidays	New financial year
May	• Eid-Ul-Fitr — Muslim festival. Bank holidays and school half-term.	
June	• Shavout — Jewish festival Martydom of Guru Arjan Dev — Sikh festival School half-term and exams.	School Tutors very busy
July	• Eid-Ul-Adha — Muslim festival. Birthday of Haile Selassi — Rastafarian festival. End of school year, people on holiday.	Many workers busy with final details of play schemes.

Table 10.1 continued

Month	Local people	Professional workers
August	• School holidays, parents fully occupied or away.	
September	• Ganeshcholth — Hindu festival. Ethiopian New Year's Day — Rastafarian festival. Rosh Hashanah — Jewish festival. School begins.	Some workers still on holiday.
October	• Rosh Hashanah, Yon Kippur, Sukkot, Shemini Atzeret Simchat Torah — Jewish festivals. Birthday of Muhammad — Muslim festival. Navaratari Puja — Hindu festival. Last week may be half-term.	Review budgets. Prepare next year's budgets.
November	• Birthday of Guru Nanak — Sikh festival. Divali — Hindu, Sikh festivals. First week may be half-term.	
December	• Christmas. Martyrdom of Guru Tegh Bahadur — Sikh festival. School holidays.	School teachers very busy.

(Based on 1989, to be adapted as date/local circumstances require. Calendars of major religions vary annually. Up-to-date calendars can be found in many annual diaries.)

11 Adult learning

Using suitable methods

Adults learn through sharing information, skills and experience, and a course which does not actively encourage sharing is likely to lose its participants. It is important to create an adult learning environment and not a schoolroom environment. As tutors, project organisers will need to be sensitive to the possibility that some participants will be reluctant to write things down, or experience difficulty in reading. Instructions will need to be given in a number of ways, both visual and oral. Content and methods must be monitored rigorously for cultural acceptability and appropriateness. For example, COPE used to recommend the use of a map and map pins to identify local resources in the first session on 'getting to know your neighbourhood'. However, on a course for Asian women, it became apparent that 'maps' are not the way Asian women 'see' neighbourhoods, and some may be unfamiliar with the concept.

A course of this nature, therefore, does not lend itself to 'traditional' teaching. It can be difficult to strike the right balance for what is likely to be a varied group of participants. There should be a mix of discussions, practical demonstrations, and individual fact-finding missions. It is important that the course tutors are responsive to people without allowing the course to lose direction. It is unwise to cram in too much. Instead, participants should be made aware that there are professionals and experts who can supply more details. Tutors should concentrate on giving participants the confidence to use such external resources rather than trying to resolve all the issues themselves. The methods used should create the variety necessary in the course, whilst facilitating the work being done.

Active participation techniques: some examples

The examples below illustrate some of the possibilities.[1]

Buzz sessions

After listening to a short talk or some similar input, course participants are asked to turn to their neighbour and share their impressions for 5 minutes. Brief reports from these 'buzz sessions' are then brought back to a general session. This can be a useful guide as to what participants have understood. Buzz sessions can also be used as warm-up sessions, with each person saying something and the tutor writing it up on a flip-chart.

Brainstorming

Participants are asked to shout out ideas or names as they occur to them relating to the issue being discussed. This technique is a good way of extracting a great many ideas from individual participants or groups in a short time. The basic rule is that no one is allowed to question or contradict anything that is said until everyone has expressed her/his views.

Specific task groups

A small group of participants (three or four people) is given a specific problem or topic to discuss and resolve relating to situations family-group workers may experience, such as 'How would you deal with a parent who, in your view, inappropriately disciplines their child during sessions?', or 'How would you optimise the benefit of having one elderly person in a group of young parents?' These small groups have the advantage of allowing easy communication and more 'air time' for individual participants.

Role playing

Participants are asked to act out a role that has been carefully explained to them with written details. This allows participants to practice skills and explore ideas and feelings in a simulation of a real-life experience, and extract learning from it. It is important to allow time for 'de-roling' at the end. Role-play is best introduced as a game, and should not be used in a course until participants are comfortable with each other and willing to 'play'.

Games

Games can be used as 'icebreakers', to provide lively sessions which also encourage learning. They are equally useful for defusing tense situations. For example, participants could be asked to describe each other as particular animals. This opens up discussions about perceptions and assumptions about each other's behaviour, but all in a spirit of good humour.

The name game is a useful first-day opener.

Procedures

1. Seat the group in a circle.
2. Choose a person from anywhere in the room to introduce him/herself, e.g. Q. 'Say who you are'; A. 'I am Mary Jones'.
3. Ask Mary Jones to 'pass it on' to the left/right.
4. That person introduces her/himself, and also says who the first person is e.g. 'I am Bill Smith and this is Mary Jones'.
5. The third person is then asked to remember the first two people's names in addition to giving her/his own, i.e. 'I am Betty Bruce, this is Bill Smith and that is Mary Jones'.
6. Every person, in turn, gives his/her name and repeats the names of everyone who has been introduced previously until the circle is completed.

It is important to maintain the 'game spirit', and not insist on 'playing by the rules':

- Accept 'cheating', for example, when people start to write down names or tick them off against a membership list — anything to assist recognition should be encouraged.
- The chain can be broken by stopping at the half-way point and re-starting at the other end, thus building a new chain back to the point where it previously stopped. This, if done without previous warning, usually causes a great deal of laughter — relief for some, sudden panic for others.
- It is useful for the tutor to take part. This helps to establish his/her identification with the group.

When games are introduced, there may be initial resistance, which is usually quickly dispelled once the game is under way. Such games can help people who are shy about speaking in a large group to overcome their inhibitions. Although a game may take up 20–30 minutes in a large group, games are never time wasting — if the wider purpose of group integration is kept in mind.

Debates

The best ideas do not always win out in the debating forum, and 'winning' can become more important than rational discussion. But, asking groups to discuss opposing views does help clarify ideas and enhance learning.

Homework

Course participants will be asked to do a certain amount of homework throughout the course at the discretion of the tutor. Homework includes, for example, visiting services in the community with which participants have had no previous dealings, completing a list of the facilities and equipment needed by a family group, thinking through areas for discussion, and making notes to bring to the following session. The intention here is to keep motivation high, to increase learning, and to facilitate links between sessions.

References

1. For further discussion, and a wide range of examples, see R. Douglas *et al.* (1988) *Helping People Work Together: A Guide to Participative Working Practices*. London NISW.

12   Planning the course

Planning and preparing the course

The organisers should plan and prepare the course together. The essential elements in the planning are:

- Define aims.
- Define objectives (which must be able to be tested).
- Write a syllabus (outline content).

Organisers should then move on to the preparation:

- Devise how the work is to be undertaken.
- Produce individual session plans.
- Determine how to evaluate the course.

The planning outline presented here is not meant to be prescriptive but more a guide to the general areas a course should cover, and in what time. The detail should be determined at the preparation stage by the project organisers, relevant to the particular participants and locality in which the course is to run. Each project is different, and the course has therefore to be thought out for that particular project. In devising how the work is to be undertaken, it is important to recognise that course participants are the course material. Therefore, there must be gaps within 'tailor-made' sessions to accommodate their skills, needs and personal development.

Planning schedule

Duration 16 weeks (32 two-hour sessions, twice weekly).

Aims of the family-group preparation course

To develop and prepare potential family-group workers to set up and
run family groups in their own neighbourhood.

The objectives of the family-group preparation course are to develop:
Stage 1 (12 sessions/24 hours) Knowledge of neighbourhood and
community resources, formal and informal, e.g.

● Local characteristics
● Local networks
● Local groups
● Local resources
● Statutory services.

by building on participants' *practical knowledge.*

Stage 2 (10 sessions/20 hours)   Self-development and the practical skills
used in family groups, e.g.

● Self-awareness
● Awareness of others
● Self-confidence
● Being trusted by others
● Listening and observing skills
● Working with under-fives
● Motivating adults
● Demonstrating activities
● Parenting skills
● Home-making skills
● Craft skills
● Welfare rights.

by building on participants' *personal qualities and practical skills.*

Stage 3 (10 sessions/20 hours) Skills used in setting up and running
family groups, e.g.

● Negotiating premises/equipment
● Recruiting members
● Organising and planning
● Budgeting
● Keeping records.

by building on participants' *life experience.*

The course in stages: outlines

Stage 1

12 sessions (24 hours in 6 weeks)

Here the focus is on drawing out participants' knowledge of, and information about, their neighbourhood, and building a group identity. Activities include asking participants to visit unfamiliar places in their neighbourhood and bring back information. It is important to demonstrate that family-group work is active, that it starts from what people know, and is about sharing. Towards the end of this stage, participants should be integrated sufficiently as a group to start exploring more sensitive areas such as child development, family life, and friendship.

- Concentrate on getting the participants to gel as a group.
- Develop participants' self-confidence by building on, and increasing, their local knowledge.
- Move towards more sensitive areas, e.g. family life, child development.

Initial welcome

Aim To help people relax, and to clarify a group understanding about the aims of the course and the project. There should be personal introductions, talks on administrative details, and explanations of the purpose and structure of the course overall.

Content Participants will need this space to clarify issues and to influence the design of future sessions. (Ensure they are happy with the creche arrangements.)

Getting to know the neighbourhood

Aim To start drawing on participants' own knowledge, to help the group to share the information.

Content Information about local resources and facilities put forward by course participants.

Homework Finding out about local services supporting families.

Activity workshop

Aim   To help the group gel.

Learning objective   To identify different family patterns and lifestyles in the community.

Content   Course participants are asked to bring their own photos, and give contributions on their day-to-day lives.

Homework   Visiting places families use but which individual participants have never been to. Participants are briefed to explain at the next group session how welcoming the chosen venue is, how helpful the people were, and what use could be made of the place by a family group.

Families and health

Aim   To raise awareness of the importance of positive health care and increase information about what help is available.

Learning objective   To develop a knowledge of what constitutes good health.

Content   Sharing health care ideas and/or informative discussion.

Homework   Participants think about the last time they asked for help with health matters, who they asked, how did they feel? This is discussed at the next session.

Asking for and receiving help

Aim   To raise awareness about the different ways of asking for help.

Learning objective   To develop the ability to recognise the different ways people communicate their needs.

Content   Body language, communication skills, listening skills.

Stage 2

10 sessions (20 hours in 5 weeks)

These sessions should enable participants to experience the value of simple activities in creating a welcoming, sharing, learning environment. There should be opportunities to discuss the help people need at different times in their lives, and who is the best person to give it. Speakers from the organisation with whom the potential family-group workers will be liaising should be invited. It is important to brief the speakers well about the aims of the course and the family groups. There should be a constructive learning atmosphere by this stage.

- Develop participants' self-confidence and awareness of self and others.
- Develop group-work skills: listening, communicating, under-standing of how groups work.
- Develop confidence in using practical activities in groups.
- Start bringing in outside speakers.

What helps adults learn and grow in self-confidence

Aim   To raise awareness of the importance of creating achievable goals for vulnerable people. The session should raise awareness of the importance of identifying the abilities and expectations of group members, so that people experience success and achievement. The course should mirror, for participants, the emphasis on the value of activities in a family group.

Learning objective   To identify the factors which assist adults in personal growth and learning.

Content   Activity workshop and discussion.

Working in a family group

Aim   To recognise some of the difficulties involved in group work, and to explore how to handle them in a positive way.

Learning objective   To develop the ability to identify potential difficulties in a group, and to discuss ways of defusing them.

Content   The ground rules of a family group, confidentiality, identification of the needs of the group and individuals, preventing cliques, handling conflict.

Homework   Participants plan an activity suitable for a family group, which can then be demonstrated on the course in an activity workshop.

The needs of 3−5 year olds (assuming this is a target group of the project)

Aim To raise awareness of the development and play of 3−5 year old children.

Learning objective To list provision for the under-fives, and demonstrate the importance of play.

Content Review of the course participants' knowledge and information. Talk by under-eights' advisor.

The importance of children as family-group members

Aim To emphasise that children are full members of a family group, and that their membership means a positive learning and sharing experience for everyone.

Learning objective To explain why children are important members of a family group, and to define the roles and tasks of the group, the play and assistant play leaders in relation to the children.

Content A review of participants' information and experience, with new information introduced where needed. Methods of working with children and parents. Work focused on attitudes to nurturing and discipline.

Working as a team

Aim To look at how aims can be achieved through teamwork.

Learning objective To explain the nature of teamwork in family groups.

Content What is a team, what does teamwork mean, how do teams work?

Stage 3

10 sessions (20 hours in 5 weeks)

By this stage in the course, the participants should have derived enough satisfaction to find the course worthwhile in its own right, and they will be considering whether they want to go any further with the project. Participants thus need sessions on what family groups can offer, the funders' expectations, the tasks of the group and play leaders, recruiting and welcoming the members, premises and equipment, diary-keeping and basic book-keeping.

- Family group aims, what the groups offer
- Recruitment of members
- Premises
- Tasks of group workers
- Record-keeping

The practicalities of setting up a family group

Aim To prepare participants for the practical tasks of setting up a family group, and to give information.

Learning objective To list the practical considerations of setting up a family group.

Content Premises — suitability, safety. Negotiation for use of rooms and storage. Equipment for adults and children — what is needed and how to get it.

Other people's experience of setting up a family group

Aim To reassure participants that other people similar to them have succeeded, and to demonstrate how skills and information from the preparation course can be used.

Learning objective To encourage participants to recognise their own skills and abilities to set up family groups.

Content COPE video of family groups in action. Talk by experienced family-group leader.

Recruitment of family-group members from the neighbourhood

Aim To start course participants thinking about recruitment of members.

Learning objective To allow participants to demonstrate their increased knowledge of, and skills in, recruiting family-group members.

Content Discussion of who, why, how, where and when?

Recruitment of family-group members through referrals

Aim To stress the importance of links between family-group workers and professional agencies, discuss the best ways of handling referrals, and explore the expectations which professional workers and family-group workers have of each other.

Learning objective To list agencies that might refer family-group members, and to develop recognition of the importance of establishing alliances.

Content Information about agencies and links made during the course, and how to use them.

Support for the project and for family groups

Aim To reassure course participants that there will be continuing support and training.

Learning objective To encourage participants to accept the needs for support and in-service training.

Content Information about the form support will take, and about in-service training. Statement of the expectations of the funders that the family-group workers attend support meetings and in-service training. Course participants' views and expressed needs.

Where do we go from here

Aim To give course participants information about what will be expected of them, in terms of record-keeping, book-keeping, etc, about the contract between family-group workers and funders, and about knowledge and skills in filling in application forms.

Learning objective To demonstrate how to apply for a job, showing knowledge of what will be expected of family-group workers.

Content Information on job descriptions and application forms, and practical exercises.

Review of course

Aim To help course participants wind up the course on their own terms, giving feed-back to tutors, and highlighting future support and training needs.

Learning objective   To identify the skills and knowledge acquired on the course.

Content   Review of course content.

13 Employing family-group workers

Employment processes

Throughout the course, the project organisers have both the overt role of tutors, and the covert role of potential employer representatives. As the course draws to a close, the two roles merge. However, the role of tutor should not be allowed to become secondary. The project organisers will have planned, before the course started, when to begin implementing the employment processes, and how. The need to be very clear about what these processes are, and which role is relevant at which stage.

The processes are:

assessment

recommendation

selection

appointment.

Assessment (Project organisers as tutors)

The course has been designed to test and build on the skills and qualities needed in the family group workers. Throughout the course, at each session, the organisers will have been assessing participants' attitudes, potential qualities and skills. Inevitably, the two organisers may not see eye to eye. It is essential that sessional records are kept for each participant.

These should record:

- attendance
- punctuality
- whether preparation has been done
- confidence
- enjoyment
- willingness to join in and help others
- other attributes considered important.

It should be agreed whether to keep separate or joint records.

Recommendation

(Project organisers as tutors making recommendations to the future employers about participants' suitability)

Depending on how the weekly assessments are recorded, there will be either two sets of recommendations that need to be agreed and negotiated, or a joint effort on a final formal assessment. The handling of the final assessments and recommendations should be agreed before the course starts:

- Are they to be verbal or written?
- If written, what format?
- Who will they be sent to?
- Will participants see their records and the recommendations only on request, or as part of the training?

It is wise to include a third more independent party (perhaps the supervisor) to act as a sounding board when final joint recommendations are made.

Selection

(Project organisers as agents of the future employer)

Selection is extremely tricky, and can easily be confused with recommendation and appointment. Plenty of counselling time is needed:

- There will be people who are unsuitable as family-group workers, but who would be very good at other things. Intuitively they will know this, but they may need help in finding out what is right for them. As tutors, organisers can help this process of self-selection.
- There will be some who are ideal, but who need encouragement to put themselves forward.

- There will be some who want to be group leaders but who would be better as play leaders, and vice versa, who will need guidance.
- There will be some who need counselling out altogether.

People who work well together for the benefit of the group members need to be matched.

Whether all participants have the right to go forward to interview, or only those who are recommended, must be clearly understood at the outset of the course. Project organisers must be clear about the criteria for recommendation from the start, and give early warning to participants who are unlikely to be recommended.

Checking records of offences for potential group leaders and assistants may be advisable but can act as a considerable delaying factor to starting the group.

It is held that, because it is only a 2-hour session, and because parents are present, or in the building all the time, there is less reason why there should be police checks. *In reality*, all the authorities and voluntary organisations who have set up family groups did negotiate with the police and did have checks on the play leaders. It is widely accepted as good practice. What is more, because of the quality of the training, the play leaders fairly quickly get involved in additional work where the parents are not in attendance. Police checks take time, and, where relations are bad with an authority, the police can be extremely obstructive. For example: in one northern area, the checks took 5 months. The poor relations were known about but nothing was done until too late. . . that is in terms of negotiating at the right level so things could move forward once the people had been appointed. This delay cost the project three excellent workers, who found other things to do, and 5 months' funding. The same is true of health checks and negotiations with the health authority.

Appointment

(Project organisers as agents of the future employer)

Organisers must be fully conversant with the relevant employment policies, which will dictate the method of appointment at the end of the course. The procedures and implications should be explained fully to participants both at commencement, and towards the end, of the course. If play leaders are included in the appointment process, their appointment should proceed in parallel with, or immediately after, that of the leaders.

Project organisers are the link between management and the potential family-group workers. It is their responsibility to:

- advise on the timing of interviews
- advise who should be present
- ensure that references, medical and police checks are sensitively and efficiently handled
- provide recommendations and/or reports on the applicants based on their work whilst on the course.

Organisers are in a difficult position. As tutors, they have worked closely with the course participants and made a range of relationships, setting up certain expectations. Openness and honesty with participants about their progress or lack of it towards a positive recommendation for appointment will reduce any resentment felt by disappointed applicants towards the project organisers. Such behaviour also models for participants what is expected of family-group workers in relation to the group members.

Sample job descriptions

Job description for the family-group leader

Aim of the family group To create personal growth through the sharing of skills, information and ideas, thereby increasing individual members' self-confidence and joy in life.

Objectives of the family group:

1. To undertake activities appropriate to the members' needs, both as individuals and within the group as a whole.
2. To provide and encourage exchange of information.
3. To create opportunities for members to learn from each other and share skills.
4. To provide opportunities for members to meet, and discuss their concerns, with experts when appropriate.
5. To raise members' awareness of other social and educational opportunities, and to encourage members to move on to them.
6. To develop links between formal caring services and members.

The family-group leader carries overall responsibility for the group and is accountable to the project organiser. S/he will be expected to undertake the following tasks:

1. To ensure that the play-group is experienced as an integral and important part of the family group by:
   (a) regularly discussing the group's development with the play leader.
   (b) ensuring that the play leader has resources.

2. To take overall responsibility for the running of the family group.
3. To make arrangements for a substitute if s/he is unable to attend.
4. To inform the project organiser if s/he is unable to open the group at any time due to sickness.
5. To recruit the membership so that there is a mix of age, skills, and needs.
6. To follow up members who have not been attending.
7. To ensure an appropriate programme of activities, speakers, films and outings.
8. To keep a record of membership, attendance and finances.
9. To complete a monthly record sheet for the funders.
10. To liaise with the caretaker, centre manager, headteacher, or landlord over the use of the premises.
11. To link up, and liaise, with the voluntary and statutory agencies.
12. To attend monthly support meetings and in-service training.

Job description for the family-group play leader

The play leader has a major responsibility to work with the group leader on behalf of the children, to ensure that the aims and objectives of the group, as defined in the family-group leader's job description, are met.

The play leader will be accountable to the group leader in carrying out the following tasks:

1. To provide a good standard of play for the children.
2. To keep a record of the children's attendance.
3. To plan a programme of play activities for the children which, from time to time, will include adults.
4. To advise the group leader on the resources needed in the play-group.
5. To be responsible for the play equipment (its storage, repair, cleanliness), and for the ordering of new materials as necessary.
6. To help and advise parents on child development, play and local services.
7. To complete a monthly record sheet for the funders.
8. To inform the family-group leader if s/he is unable to work in the group at any time due to sickness or ill health.
9. To arrange for a substitute if necessary.
10. To be involved in the recruitment of members.
11. To attend monthly support meetings and in-service training days.

Job description for the assistant play leader

The assistant play leader will work with the play leader to fulfil the aims and objectives of the family group and undertake the following tasks:

1. To assist the play leader to provide a good standard of play.
2. To assist in the play programme.
3. To assist in putting out, maintaining and putting away the play-group equipment.
4. To assist in caring for the children.
5. To offer information and advice to mothers on play services available in the area.
6. To inform the family-group leader if s/he is unable to work at any time in the group due to sickness.
7. To attend monthly support meetings and in-service training days.

Sample letter of appointment

For the family-group play leader

Dear . . . .

We are pleased to confirm your appointment as a family-group play leader. This is a sessional post and your contract will be reviewed in x months. If your work has been satisfactory, it will be renewed until the funding for the project ceases.

The main terms and conditions of your engagement are given below:

- You will be managed and supervised by the project organiser.
- You will be expected to run a play-group for 2 hours a week during school term-time, that is 37 weeks of the year. The sessional fee you will receive will be £. . . . . . per hour making a total of £. . . . . . per week. There will be an additional payment of £. . . . . . to cover the half hour's work that you will need to do before and after the group, to set up the equipment and clear away.
- You will receive a sessional rate of £. . . . . per hour for attending support meetings and in-service training. You will meet your own travelling expenses on these occasions.
- You will be expected to submit a weekly time sheet to the project organiser and will be paid monthly. The method of payment will be by arrangement with x.

- As a sessional worker, you will not be entitled to annual leave. No special salary payments or arrangements will be made in respect of Public or Bank Holidays. Neither will you be entitled to any overtime, bonus or enhanced payments.
- You will not be entitled to sick leave or sick pay, but you must inform the project organiser as early as possible when you are unfit to work.
- As a family-group worker you will gain knowledge of, or have access to, information that is confidential. It is a condition of your engagement that confidentiality must be respected.

It is planned to start setting up the groups from the week beginning . . . . Teams of workers and venues will be decided nearer this time.

. . . . has great pleasure in welcoming you to the project and looks forward to working with you.

Best wishes,

Yours sincerely

14 Guidelines for the support of family groups and family-group workers

The transition from course tutor to support worker is the final stage for the project organiser. Once the course has ended, and the family-group leaders and play leaders have been appointed, the main task for the project organiser is providing support. The group workers will rapidly gain confidence and become more independent if they are assured that they can easily contact the support worker, and that there will be a quick response.

The aims of support are:

- the maintenance of the standards set by the course
- the development and support of the family groups
- practical, professional, personal support of the family-group workers as required.

Forms of support

Personal meetings

These would be at the request of either the project organiser or the family-group worker, and would probably be concerned with giving moral support and self-confidence to the worker. These meetings would probably be requested only at the early stages of establishing a family group. They should not be allowed to become the norm.

Monthly support meetings

These meetings are usually held once a month for 2 hours, during school term-times. The meetings should include all the family-group workers in the project and the support worker. The purpose of the meetings is for the workers to share ideas, successes and problems in a mutually supportive atmosphere. The meetings should make it clear that the group workers are doing an important and relevant piece of work and are taken seriously as employees. Experience has shown that there needs to be a regular but short administrative agenda, with checks that pay claims and records are handed in, that petty cash and running funds are up to date, and that wage cheques have been paid out.

The support worker thus can keep an unobtrusive finger on the pulse, and be sure that the groups within a project are meeting the aims of the project.

Visits to the groups

The question of visits to the groups is an issue which must be understood by all concerned and handled sensitively. The problems of confidentiality and the group feeling 'inspected' have to be balanced against their need to be cared for, and the support workers' need to know what is going on. Visits to the group by other professionals need to be carefully regulated and negotiated through the support worker, group workers and members.

In-service training

In-service training in the form of one-day workshops, two or three times a year, perhaps on a specific topic, for example, 'The emotional and play needs of very young children', is vital if the group workers are to develop and grow. Without this stimulation, the groups could become sterile and repetitive. Everyone needs refreshment.

Play leaders

There is a danger of the support focusing on the role of the family group leader and omitting the play leader. This results in a lowering of morale, and frequently of standards. Play leaders may well fail to attend the support meetings because the topics are not relevant to their area of work and may begin to feel excluded and unimportant. It is through support meetings, and in-service training, that all group workers are made to feel that they are part of a team and that their work is valued by funders.

15 Monitoring, assessment and evaluation

The family-group project could easily drift in the hands of organisers experiencing conflicting demands such as a health visitor with a list of under-fives visits to make. Equally, the project could be developed successfully in the eyes of the organiser and workers but unprovable to critical new managers. Planning in monitoring and evaluation at the outset can avoid the difficulties which may arise as a consequence.

To monitor the project requires the gathering in of data. This could be meaningless unless the data are analyzed to produce an evaluation. It is always tempting to gather in all data available. The volume becomes unmanageable, and the evaluation never takes place.

So consideration of what data and why that data, is advisable.

The data to be gathered in are likely to be either quantitative e.g. how many referrals?; how many course participants?; or qualitative, e.g. what deterred referees from joining the group?; what sessions did participants find most enlightening and why? Quantitative data are simpler to gather than qualitative but can be of less use in relation to the true value and impact of the work being evaluated. Ideally, there should be a blend of the two. The *NHS and Community Care Act 1990* has introduced an emphasis on quality and the ability to evaluate it. All local authorities have 'arm's length inspection units' where 'value for money' and quality analysis will be undertaken. When preparing the project, the organisers usefully could ask staff, of such units, for their advice on approaches to a qualitative evaluation.

Points of data gathering

The area needs profile will produce considerable data some of which
can be used for monitoring the project. If the project is to focus on
young families with pre-school children then data on:

- the incidence of young families — census
- those held on the health visitor's register
- those known to schools and social services

may give a base figure which justifies targeting this group. It may
be compared with national averages to give a context to the occur-
rence of young families in the area. In reality, these figures will give
no real indication of the actual uptake as this will depend on local
attitudes, how the project is presented, and so forth.

If the project is running four family groups across a locality, it may
be appropriate to relate the progress of one to another. The following
may be considered.

- Keep profiles of group users, e.g. employed, lone parents.
- Keep details of the activities.
- Keep records of the sessions completed.
- Take a trawl of users' views on arrival, 6 weeks later, and at end
  of involvement.

Any variations can form the basis of workers' meetings and supervision sessions. Whilst one is not aspiring to uniformity, variations
may indicate difficulties afoot or excellent ideas to be used
elsewhere. If users are actively involved in the groups, then variety
is inevitable and appropriate.

The numbers of unfilled places may act as a useful measure to
assess the group's relevance to local people. The places may not be
filled every week but if, over a 3-week period, only three out of eight
people turn up, there is an indication that action is needed. This may
be by contacting the absent five. Equally, it may require discussion
with the core of three. Are they acting as an exclusive group? How
best can they share the responsibility for engaging other participants?

Considering success

At commencement, it will be important to determine what would
constitute success. Whilst the organiser may have some ideas on this,
the inclusion of potential members' views will make the evidence
more comprehensive. Their views can be asked at the point when

they agree they would like to become group members. Some views may be very individual, e.g. 'success to me would be gaining enough confidence to go to a job interview'. Some could be aggregated to give a broader indicator.

The Course

At commencement, participants may be asked to write, on an index card, their expectations of the course and their personal needs in relation to becoming a group leader. These can then be stored by the course organiser to be used at the end of the course. This can be repeated mid-way through the course.

The final session of the course includes a review. Participants can be asked again to complete a card. On one side, they can write their comments on course content and, on the other, their comments on how the sessions were run. When aggregated by the organisers, this may provide a snapshot view only. Many participants will not be able to distinguish one session from another by this stage. Having done this general review course, participants can be given back their original 'expectation cards' and be asked to comment on the degree to which their needs and expectations were fulfilled and the extent to which they changed during the course. This will provide useful data in relation to individual participants and, if aggregated, may indicate weak spots in the course, and unmet needs to be planned for.

If the organisers decide they wish to evaluate the course benefits to those who do not become group organisers, then a 3 – 6 month follow-up contact will be needed. This may indicate usefully the broader value of such a course for local people, or not. If such a value was proven, it may be appropriate to set up courses, suitably adjusted, outside the context of the family-group project.

This follow-up can be undertaken by telephone (records of addresses and telephone numbers will need to be retained) or by personal call. Whilst a letter could be sent, the response is likely to be very low. If this information is being tokenistically more than gathered, then effort has to be put in.

The family group

The group and play leaders' weekly reports are a rich source of data.

Short-term impact This may be indicated best by the numbers attending the group compared to those interested and those saying they would attend. A drop-off through these stages is to be expected but the end result should still be a viable group.

A second measure could be to look at the range and incidence of activities undertaken by the group. This may include a secondary measure, as the group progresses, such as the number of events arranged by members rather then by the organisers.

A third option would be to record the content of discussion, both spontaneous and planned. Over time, one could look at the extent to which spontaneous discussion increases as well as the level of discussion/conversation overall.

A record could be kept of the subject areas of discussion. This would indicate member interests and personal use of the group. Also indicated would be the extent to which the 'difficult' areas such as child-care problems versus the best shop to buy food at are being incorporated into the group.

Long-term impact The assessment of longer-term impacts is more complex and is often neglected. It is all too tempting to feel that things are going well in the sessions and that that is enough. However, remembering the aims and objectives of the group, some longer-term measures are necessary:

- Which activities are members involved in outside the group which are an extension of group involvement, e.g. shopping trips with other members, job applications, mutual child sitting?
- Which members actively decide to terminate attendance due to their own personal growth?
- In which ways would members see their quality of life as improved?
- Have members encouraged others to join?
- Have attendances at child health clinics increased (if an issue)?
- Have parent – teacher contacts increased (if an issue)?
- Are immunisations up to date (if an issue)?
- Have referrals to social services at crisis point decreased?

Some of these measures of change may be difficult to connect to just the family group. There will be other influences. Whilst monitoring cannot be a perfect science, it provides at least the basis for justifying continuance, or expansion, or closure.

The analysis of the data gathered is a powerful process. Depending upon the values, attitudes and belief in family groups, those people analysing can bias their results accordingly. It will be for an astute manager/supervisor to pick this up. What is claimed of a family group should appear rational, balanced and fair to a reasonable person.

The evaluation may be undertaken by an identified individual who could be the organiser, the manager or the supervisor. Instead of, or as well as, this consideration may be given to material being analysed within the worker meetings or within the steering group, where one exists. Whatever conclusions are generated, they should be shared with workers, users and perhaps funders. If well recorded and stored, they can also contribute to a portfolio which could be made available to those setting up family-group projects afresh. Once one can show what has been achieved, it becomes easier to justify the next project.

Appendix: A family group in action

The group profile (One of three in the project)

30 members

Referral comments

10 with depression
6 ex-hospital patients
4 on drugs
3 lone parents
1 child abuse
5 new to area, isolated
1 abortion
1 miscarriage
1 became a widow
1 post-natal depression

Some members' stories

Margaret

Margaret's son has had meningitis. John is 3 years old and had been, in her words, 'a beautiful toddler'. One side of his body is now growing visibly faster than the other. He has had to relearn how to move, sit, walk, feed and talk. Margaret has coped alone with this. Margaret needs acceptance and emotional support and uses the family group for both. 'The family group is a place where I can be honest and say what the cost is to me and how the grief feels.' But the family group also provides her with practical support.

It was a great healing factor that John could come to a play-group where he was welcomed. He established a friendship with 'one little mate' who showed incredible patience and concern, though this friendship fell off because the able child moved into a stage of rapid development and no longer waited for his 'mate'.

However, the whole group has become reflective about disability and has identified deafness as one of the worst. They asked Nancy, the support worker, to find out about sign language classes that are run for the deaf, and whether they could join them. They thought their presence might hurt or embarrass the deaf people — perhaps a class just for the group? Nancy would like a workshop.

Jane

Jane has lost a sister and is coping substantially alone with her three children. Her father-in-law is in hospital, dying of cancer, her mother-in-law is in a wheelchair, and husband is away a lot. She feels bitterly resentful and hurt. Jane uses the group as a place to talk about how she feels as well as for warm support. Quite a few group members are now having problems with parents growing older. So Jane, by expressing her difficulties, is opening up discussion relevant to many group members.

Geraldine

Geraldine is a 'difficult' member, and it has been hard work to keep the group around her at times, because she continually demands attention for her succession of problems. Her husband ran away with her social worker the day before she came out of hospital with her second baby. He has now remarried and lives as far away as possible, in Scotland. Over the summer holidays, Geraldine's 10 year-old daughter went to stay with him. There was no communication until 3 days after school started, when a letter arrived from the daughter saying she had more in common with her father and would be staying with him. Geraldine, however, has now learned self-reliance, and has taken legal advice, etc on her own. She is quite calm and commonsensical. Most important of all, she is not bending everyone's ears and making sure she is the centre of the stage in the group sessions.

Barbara

Barbara lost her baby last year and is pregnant again. The expected date of birth is the same day as the death of the first child. She has convinced herself that the new baby will be a reincarnation of the first, and came to the group to talk about it. Iris, the group leader, dispelled this notion as best she could. Afterwards, a visitor to the group thanked Iris for taking this commonsense approach. The visitor was a trained health visitor attached to Barbara for the duration of the pregnancy. Barbara had insisted that the health visitor should come to the group to see the support and advice that the group provides.

Changes in the community

The little local shops have changed ownership and no longer provide the meeting places they used to. Instead, the focus is an enormous Tesco's which sells just about everything and is expensive. All it needs is a coffee bar to make it a real community centre. The problem is that it puts subtle pressure on people and makes them feel they aren't good enough unless they live up to the lifestyle that the shop projects.

Some of the members of the three groups know each other outside the project as well. They meet at Tesco's, and keep in touch in other ways. The groups are quite close because the leaders have worked at supporting each other and providing joint opportunities for members, such as badminton, basket-making, swimming, a child development course, etc.

Nancy, the support worker, sees the family groups as the beginning of the building of a community. She has also started in the area:

- badminton funded by adult education
- badminton with a local group of people
- a swimming group on Friday evenings.

The latest venture is a community drama group to which Nancy is recruiting children, men, women, adolescents, and the older people. She tries to get two people at least from each of the three groups to be members of another group, so that, over a period of time, all the members of all the groups will get to know each other and share events such as summer outings, etc. So, the family group summer outing this year will include people from both the badminton and swimming groups, who are not members of the family group, and would never wish to be, but none the less understand it, respect it, and would refer people to it.

Bibliography

Addison, C. (1988) *Planning Investigative Projects: A Workbook for Social Services Practitioners*, London: National Institute for Social Work (NISW).

Bond, T. (1986) *Games for Social and Life Skills*, London: Hutchinson.

Brown, A. *et al.* (1988) *Training Social Workers for Groupwork*, London: NISW.

Egan, G. (1986) *The Skilled Helper*, Brook Cole.

Galinsky, M. and Schopler, J.H. (1985) 'Patterns of entry and exit in open-ended groups' *Social Work with Groups*, 8(2).

Garland, J. A. and Kolodny, R. L. (1972) 'Characteristics and Resolution of Scapegoating', in Bernstein, S. (ed.), *Further Explorations in Group-work*, London: Bookstall Publications.

Gibbons, J. (1990) *Family Support and Prevention*, HMSO.

Gorrell-Barnes, G. (1984) *Working with Families*, Basingstoke: Macmillan.

Kelly, D., Payne, C. and Warwick J. (1990) *Making National Vocational Qualifications Work for Social Care*, London: NISW.

Laughary, J. W. and Hopson, B. (1979) *Producing Workshops, Seminars and Short Courses — A Trainers Handbook*, Association Press.

Lindenfield, G. and Adams, R. (1984) *Problem-Solving through Self-Help Groups*, Ilkley: Self-Help Associates.

Lovell, R. B. (1987) *Adult Learning*, Routledge Reprinted.

McCaughan, N. (1977) 'Group behaviour: some theories for practice' in Briscoe, C. and Thomas, D. N. (eds), *Community Work: Learning and Supervision*, London: George Allen & Unwin.

Maple, F. F. (1977) *Shared Decision Making*, London: Sage Publications.

Payne, C. and Scott, T. (1990) *Developing Supervision in Teams, in Field and Residential Social Work*, London: NISW, Reprinted.

Pfeiffer, J. W. and Jones, J. E. (1974–1983) *A Handbook of Structured Experiences for Human Relations Training*, Vol i – ix University Associates.

Schopler, J. H. and Galinsky, M. (1984) 'Meeting practice needs: conceptualizing the open-ended group', *Social Work with Groups*, 7(2).

Silverman, P. (1980) *Mutual Help Groups*, London: Sage.

Steiner, I. D. (1974) *Task-performing Groups*, Morristown, NJ: General Learning Press.

Thomas, D.N. (1978) 'Journey into the acting community: experiences of learning and change in community groups' in N. McCaughan (ed.), *Group Work: Learning and Practice*, London: George Allen & Unwin.

Vorrath, H. H. and Brendtro, L. K. (1984 edn.) *Positive Peer Culture*, Chicago: Aldine.

Whitaker, D. S. (1976) 'Some conditions for effective work with groups', *British Journal of Social Work*, **5**, (**4**) 423 – 39.